Jen,
Cook,
eat, and be happy.

Love,
C, I & B

# AMERICAN
# HOME COOKING

THE AMERICAN FAMILY COOKING LIBRARY

# AMERICAN
# HOME COOKING

### FRANCES CLEARY

SMITHMARK

This edition published in 1993
by SMITHMARK Publishers Inc.
16 East 32nd Street
New York
NY 10016
USA

SMITHMARK books are available for bulk purchase for sales promotion
and premium use. For details write or call the manager of special sales,
SMITHMARK Publishers Inc.
16 East 32nd Street
New York
NY 10016
(212) 532-6600

Reprinted in 1995

Publisher: Joanna Lorenz
Project Editor: Carole Clements
Copy Editor: Norma MacMillan
Designer: Sheila Volpe
Photographer: Amanda Heywood
Food Styling: Frances Cleary, Carole Handslip,
steps by Nicola Fowler

Printed and bound in Hong Kong

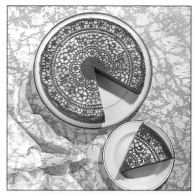

# CONTENTS

~

| | |
|---|---|
| INTRODUCTION | 6 |
| SOUPS, SANDWICHES & APPETIZERS | 8 |
| FISH & SEAFOOD | 40 |
| MEAT & POULTRY | 66 |
| PASTA, PIZZA & GRAINS | 112 |
| SALADS, VEGETABLES, EGGS & CHEESE | 144 |
| BREADS, CAKES, PIES & COOKIES | 184 |
| HOT & COLD DESSERTS | 222 |
| INDEX | 252 |

# INTRODUCTION

~

American home cooking means putting together weekday meals and having friends and relatives over for dinner. It means rummaging through notebooks and file-card boxes to find a special aunt's recipe for roast turkey or a neighbor's elegant chocolate cake.

In preparing this book, we brought together old-time favorites and added new ideas, which reflect the appearance of exotic and specialty ingredients in local markets, and the evolution of the way we eat. But here each recipe is brought to life, every step of the way, in pictures.

It's easy to learn basic cooking know-how with the help of this book. With pictures to guide you at every stage, even a beginner can cook meals with confidence. For the experienced cook, the step-by-step photographs serve as memory-joggers. You will practically be able to cook at a glance from a treasury of over 200 recipes.

To start off a meal or sit down to a simple one, there are chunky soups and cold ones, plus sandwiches to eat with both hands, and appetizers plain and fancy. The seafood recipes take full advantage of our fish- and shellfish-stocked lakes and coastal waters. For many people, meat and poultry are the heart of a meal, and the choice here includes long-simmered as well as speedy dishes. If you have shifted the balance of your diet to grains and fresh produce, you will find recipes for pasta and pizza, beans and vegetables. Baking may be a luxury these days, but with the particulars spelled out, it requires less effort to fill the kitchen with fragrant smells.

Here is American family cooking in all its variety. From the category of foods that mean home and comfort, we chose such standbys as macaroni and cheese, chicken potpie and peach cobbler. Sometimes we put a twist on the basics, offering cornish game hens with cranberry sauce, guacamole cheese-burgers and chocolate brownie sundaes. Regional and immigrant specialties are represented with tacos, jambalaya, calzone, pork with sauerkraut, and more.

The only thing that's missing in *American Home Cooking* are the aromas. Still, there's no substitute for experience. Only you know the quirks of your oven and how to get the best from your equipment. Setting out all the ingredients before beginning and measuring accurately is just sound culinary practice. Even perfect technique won't remedy lack of flavor. Good ingredients are essential to good cooking. Stay in tune with the seasons, choosing fruits and vegetables at their peak. And remember to taste and adjust the seasoning, if necessary, before serving.

Our hectic schedules leave us less time in the kitchen these days, but we hope this book rekindles the pleasures of family cooking. Homemade can make a comeback in your house with the help of *American Home Cooking*.

# SOUPS, SANDWICHES & APPETIZERS

~

*Here are soups smooth and creamy, icy and refreshing, or hearty, to start a meal or be a meal in themselves; tempting sandwiches, both hot and cold; and sumptuous party fare.*

# Winter Vegetable Soup

**SERVES 8**

1 medium-size head of Savoy cabbage, quartered and cored

2 tablespoons corn oil

4 carrots, thinly sliced

2 celery stalks, thinly sliced

2 parsnips, diced

6 cups chicken stock

3 medium-size potatoes, diced

2 zucchini, sliced

1 small red bell pepper, seeded and diced

2 cups cauliflower florets

2 tomatoes, seeded and diced

½ teaspoon fresh thyme leaves or ¼ teaspoon dried thyme

2 tablespoons chopped fresh parsley

salt and pepper

**1** Slice the cabbage quarters into thin strips across the leaves.

**2** ▲ Heat the oil in a large saucepan. Add the cabbage, carrots, celery, and parsnips and cook 10–15 minutes over medium heat, stirring frequently.

**3** Stir the stock into the vegetables and bring to a boil. Skim off any foam that rises to the top.

**4** ▲ Add the potatoes, zucchini, bell pepper, cauliflower and tomatoes with the herbs, and salt and pepper to taste. Bring back to a boil. Reduce the heat to low, cover the pan, and simmer until the vegetables are tender, 15–20 minutes.

# Fresh Tomato Soup

**SERVES 4**

2 tablespoons butter or margarine

1 onion, chopped

2 pounds tomatoes, quartered

2 carrots, chopped

2 cups chicken stock

2 tablespoons chopped fresh parsley

½ teaspoon fresh thyme leaves or ¼ teaspoon dried thyme

⅓ cup whipping cream (optional)

salt and pepper

~ **COOK'S TIP** ~

Meaty and flavorful Italian plum tomatoes are ideal for this soup.

**1** Melt the butter or margarine in a large saucepan. Add the onion and cook until softened, about 5 minutes.

**2** ▲ Stir in the tomatoes, carrots, chicken stock, parsley and thyme. Bring to a boil. Reduce the heat to low, cover the pan, and simmer until tender, 15–20 minutes.

**3** ▼ Purée the soup in a vegetable mill. Return the puréed soup to the saucepan.

**4** Stir in the cream, if using, and reheat gently. Season with salt and pepper. Ladle into warmed soup bowls and serve hot, sprinkled with a little more thyme, if you wish.

*Winter Vegetable Soup (top), Fresh Tomato soup*

# Carrot Soup with Ginger

**SERVES 6**

2 tablespoons butter or margarine

1 onion, chopped

1 celery stalk, chopped

1 medium-size potato, chopped

1½ pounds carrots, chopped

2 teaspoons minced fresh gingerroot

5 cups chicken stock

⅓ cup whipping cream

¼ teaspoon grated nutmeg

salt and pepper

**1 ▼** Combine the butter or margarine, onion, and celery and cook until softened, about 5 minutes.

**2** Stir in the potato, carrots, gingerroot, and stock. Bring to a boil. Reduce the heat to low, cover the pan, and simmer 20 minutes.

**3 ▲** Pour the soup into a food processor or blender and process until smooth. Alternatively, use a vegetable mill to purée the soup. Return the soup to the pan. Stir in the cream and nutmeg, and add salt and pepper to taste. Reheat gently for serving.

# Minted Pea Soup

**SERVES 6**

2 tablespoons butter or margarine

1 onion, chopped

1 small head of Boston lettuce, shredded

2 pounds shelled fresh green peas or frozen peas, thawed

6 cups chicken stock

3 tablespoons chopped fresh mint

salt and pepper

¾ cup whipping cream

fresh mint sprigs, for garnishing

~ VARIATION ~

To serve cold, refrigerate the puréed soup until thoroughly chilled, 3–4 hours. Stir all the cream into the soup just before serving, or keep some to swirl onto the surface of each serving.

**1 ▲** Melt the butter or margarine in a large saucepan. Add the onion and cook until softened, about 5 minutes.

**2 ▲** Stir in the lettuce, peas, stock, and mint. Bring to a boil. Reduce the heat to low, cover the pan, and simmer 15 minutes.

**3** Pour the soup into a blender or food processor and process until smooth. Alternatively, purée the soup in a vegetable mill. Return the puréed soup to the pan. Season to taste.

**4 ▲** Stir in ½ cup of the cream and reheat gently. Ladle into bowls and serve with the remaining cream. For a decorative effect, pour a scant tablespoon of cream in a spiral design into the center of each serving, or stir it in and garnish with sprigs of mint.

*Carrot Soup with Ginger (top), Minted Pea Soup*

# Chilled Avocado and Zucchini Soup

**SERVES 6**

4 cups chicken stock

1 pound zucchini, sliced

2 large, very ripe avocados

3 tablespoons fresh lemon juice

¾ cup plain yogurt

2 teaspoons Worcestershire sauce

½ teaspoon chili powder

⅛ teaspoon sugar

dash of hot pepper sauce

salt

**1** In a large saucepan, bring the chicken stock to a boil.

**2** ▲ Add the zucchini and simmer until soft, 10–15 minutes. Let cool.

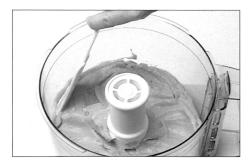

**3** ▲ Peel the avocados. Remove and discard the pits. Cut the flesh into chunks and put in a food processor or blender. Add the lemon juice and process until smooth.

**4** ▲ Using a slotted spoon, transfer the zucchini to the food processor or blender; reserve the stock. Process the zucchini with the avocado purée.

**5** ▲ Pour the avocado-zucchini purée into a bowl. Stir in the reserved stock. Add ½ cup of the yogurt, the Worcestershire sauce, chili powder, sugar, hot pepper sauce, and salt to taste. Mix well. Cover tightly and chill 3–4 hours.

**6** To serve, ladle the soup into bowls. Swirl the remaining yogurt on the surface.

# Chicken Noodle Soup

**SERVES 8**

| |
|---|
| 1 3-pound chicken, cut in pieces |
| 2 onions, quartered |
| 1 parsnip, quartered |
| 2 carrots, quartered |
| ½ teaspoon salt |
| 1 bay leaf |
| 2 allspice berries |
| 4 black peppercorns |
| 3 quarts water |
| 1 cup very thin egg noodles |
| sprigs of fresh dill, for garnishing |

**1** ▲ In a large stockpot, combine the chicken pieces, onions, parsnip, carrots, salt, bay leaf, allspice berries and peppercorns.

**2** ▲ Add the water to the pot and bring to a boil, skimming frequently.

**3** Reduce the heat to low and simmer 1½ hours, skimming occasionally.

**4** Strain the broth through a fine-mesh strainer into a bowl. Refrigerate overnight.

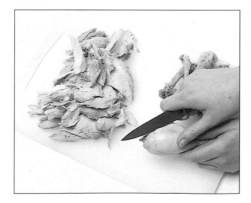

**5** ▲ When the chicken pieces are cool enough to handle, remove the meat from the bones. Discard the bones, skin, vegetables, and flavorings. Chop the chicken meat and refrigerate overnight.

**6** Remove the solidified fat from the surface of the chilled broth. Pour the broth into a saucepan and bring to a boil. Taste the broth; if a more concentrated flavor is wanted, boil 10 minutes to reduce slightly.

**7** ▲ Add the chicken meat and noodles to the broth and cook until the noodles are tender, about 8 minutes (check package directions for timing). Serve hot, garnished with dill sprigs.

# Green Bean and Parmesan Soup

**SERVES 4**

2 tablespoons butter or margarine

½ pound green beans, trimmed

1 garlic clove, minced

2 cups vegetable stock

salt and pepper

½ cup freshly grated Parmesan cheese

¼ cup light cream

2 tablespoons chopped fresh parsley

**1** Melt the butter or margarine in a medium saucepan. Add the green beans and garlic and cook 2–3 minutes over medium heat, stirring frequently.

**2 ▲** Stir in the stock and season with salt and pepper. Bring to a boil. Reduce the heat and simmer, uncovered, until the beans are tender, 10–15 minutes.

**3 ▼** Pour the soup into a blender or food processor and process until smooth. Alternatively, purée the soup in a food mill. Return to the pan. Stir in the cheese and cream. Sprinkle with the parsley and serve.

# Hearty Lentil Soup

**SERVES 6**

1 cup brown lentils

4 cups chicken stock

1 cup water

¼ cup dry red wine

1½ pounds ripe tomatoes, peeled, seeded, and chopped, or 2 cups canned crushed tomatoes

1 carrot, sliced

1 onion, chopped

1 celery stalk, sliced

1 garlic clove, minced

¼ teaspoon ground coriander

2 teaspoons chopped fresh basil, or ½ teaspoon dried basil

1 bay leaf

6 tablespoons freshly grated Parmesan cheese

**1 ▲** Rinse the lentils and discard any discolored ones and any stones.

**2 ▲** Combine the lentils, stock, water, wine, tomatoes, carrot, onion, celery, and garlic in a large saucepan. Add the coriander, basil, and bay leaf.

**3 ▼** Bring to a boil, reduce the heat to low, cover, and simmer until the lentils are just tender, 20–25 minutes, stirring occasionally.

**4** Discard the bay leaf. Ladle the soup into 6 soup bowls and sprinkle each with 1 tablespoon of the cheese.

~ **VARIATION** ~

For a more substantial soup, add about 1 cup finely chopped cooked ham for the last 10 minutes of cooking.

*Green Bean and Parmesan Soup (top), Hearty Lentil Soup*

# Black and White Bean Soup

**SERVES 8**

2 cups dry black (turtle) beans, soaked overnight

2 quarts water

6 garlic cloves, minced

2 cups dry navy or Great Northern beans, soaked overnight

6 tablespoons balsamic vinegar

4 jalapeño peppers, seeded and chopped

6 scallions, finely chopped

juice of 1 lime

¼ cup olive oil

¼ cup chopped fresh coriander (cilantro), plus more for garnishing

salt and pepper

**1** Drain and rinse the black beans. Place them in a large saucepan with half the water and garlic. Bring to a boil. Reduce the heat to low, cover the pan, and simmer until the beans are soft, about 1½ hours.

**2** Drain and rinse the white beans. Put them in another saucepan with the remaining water and garlic. Bring to a boil, cover, and simmer until soft, about 1 hour.

**3 ▲** Purée the cooked white beans in a food processor or blender. Stir in the vinegar, jalapeños, and half the scallions. Return to the saucepan and reheat gently.

**4** Purée the cooked black beans in the food processor or blender. Return to the saucepan and stir in the lime juice, olive oil, coriander, and the remaining scallions. Reheat gently.

**5 ▲** Season both soups with salt and pepper. To serve, place a ladleful of each puréed soup in each soup bowl, side by side. Swirl the two soups together with a toothpick. If liked, garnish with extra chopped fresh coriander.

# Butternut Squash Bisque

**SERVES 4**

2 tablespoons butter or margarine

2 small onions, finely chopped

1 pound butternut squash, peeled, seeded, and cubed

5 cups chicken stock

½ pound potatoes, cubed

1 teaspoon paprika

½ cup whipping cream (optional)

salt and pepper

1½ tablespoons chopped fresh chives, plus whole chives, for garnishing

**1** Melt the butter or margarine in a large saucepan. Add the onions and cook until soft, about 5 minutes.

**2 ▲** Add the squash, stock, potatoes, and paprika. Bring to a boil. Reduce the heat to low, cover the pan, and simmer until the vegetables are soft, about 35 minutes.

**3** Pour the soup into a food processor or blender and process until smooth. Return the soup to the pan and stir in the cream, if using. Season with salt and pepper. Reheat gently.

**4 ▲** Stir in the chopped chives just before serving. If liked, garnish each serving with a few whole chives.

*Black and White Bean Soup (top), Butternut Squash Bisque*

# Mozzarella, Tomato, and Pesto Sandwiches

**SERVES 4**

4 small round Italian or French bread rolls

½ cup freshly made or bottled pesto sauce

½ pound mozzarella cheese, thinly sliced

4 medium tomatoes, thinly sliced

3 tablespoons olive oil

fresh basil leaves, for garnishing

1  With a serrated knife, cut each roll open in half. Spread 1 tablespoon of pesto sauce over the cut side of each half.

2 ▲  Arrange alternating slices of mozzarella cheese and tomato on the bottom half of each roll.

3 ▲  Drizzle the olive oil over the cheese and tomatoes.

4  Replace the top half of each roll; garnish with basil leaves, if you wish.

# Salad-Stuffed Pita Pockets

**SERVES 6**

½ small head of iceberg lettuce, cut in fine strips across the leaves

½ hothouse cucumber, diced

9 cherry tomatoes, halved

2 scallions, finely chopped

½ cup crumbled feta cheese

8 black olives, pitted and chopped

6 oblong pita breads, cut in half crosswise

FOR THE DRESSING

1 small garlic clove, minced

⅛ teaspoon salt

1 teaspoon fresh lemon juice

2 tablespoons olive oil

1 teaspoon chopped fresh mint

pepper

1 ▲  In a bowl, combine the lettuce, cucumber, tomatoes, scallions, feta cheese, and olives.

2 ▲  For the dressing, combine all the ingredients in a small screwtop jar and shake well to mix.

3 ▲  Pour the dressing over the salad and toss together.

4 ▲  Gently open the pita bread halves. Fill the pockets with the salad. Serve immediately.

*Mozzarella, Tomato and Pesto Sandwiches (top), Salad-Stuffed Pita Pockets*

# Club Sandwiches

**SERVES 4**

8 bacon slices

12 slices of white bread or rectangular brioche, toasted

½ cup mayonnaise

¼–½ pound cooked chicken breast meat, sliced

8 large lettuce leaves

salt and pepper

1 beefsteak tomato, cut across in 4 slices

**1 ▼** In a heavy skillet, fry the bacon until crisp and the fat is rendered. Drain on paper towels.

**2** Lay 4 slices of toast on a flat surface. Spread them with some of the mayonnaise.

**3 ▲** Top each slice with one-quarter of the chicken and a lettuce leaf. Season with salt and pepper.

**4 ▲** Spread 4 of the remaining toast slices with mayonnaise. Lay them on top of the lettuce.

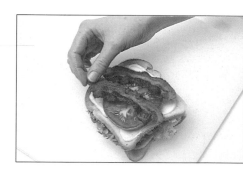

**5 ▲** Top each sandwich with a slice of tomato, 2 bacon slices, and another lettuce leaf.

**6** Spread the remaining slices of toast with the rest of the mayonnaise. Place them on top of the sandwiches, mayonnaise-side down.

**7** Cut each sandwich into four triangles and secure each triangle with a toothpick.

# Chili Dogs

**SERVES 6**

6 frankfurters

6 hot dog buns, split open

2 tablespoons butter or margarine, at room temperature

⅓ cup shredded cheddar cheese

⅓ cup chopped red onion

FOR THE CHILI

2 tablespoons corn oil

1 small onion, chopped

1 small green bell pepper, seeded and chopped

½ pound ground beef

1 cup tomato sauce

½ cup drained canned red kidney beans

2 teaspoons chili powder, or to taste

salt and pepper

**3** ▼ Stir in the tomato sauce, beans, chili powder, and salt and pepper to taste. Cover the pan and simmer 10 minutes.

**4** Meanwhile, put the frankfurters in a saucepan and cover with cold water. Bring to a boil. Remove from the heat, cover, and let stand 5 minutes.

**5** ▲ Spread both sides of each hot dog bun with the butter or margarine. Fry in a hot skillet until golden brown on both sides.

**6** To serve, put a frankfurter in each bun. Top with chili and sprinkle with cheese and onion. Serve immediately.

**1** ▲ For the chili, heat the oil in a skillet. Add the onion and green bell pepper and cook until softened, about 5 minutes.

**2** ▲ Add the beef and cook until well browned, stirring frequently and breaking up lumps with the side of a wooden spatula.

# Grilled Cheddar and Chutney Sandwiches

**SERVES 4**

3 tablespoons butter or margarine

3 large garlic cloves, minced

⅓ cup homemade or bottled mango chutney

8 slices of white bread

½ pound cheddar cheese, shredded

**1 ▲** Melt the butter or margarine in a small saucepan. Add the garlic and cook until softened but not brown, about 2 minutes, stirring. Remove from the heat.

**2 ▲** Spread the chutney on 4 slices of bread.

**3 ▲** Divide the cheese among the bread slices, spreading it evenly. Top with the remaining bread slices.

**4 ▲** Brush both sides of each sandwich with the garlic butter.

**5** Fry the sandwiches in a hot skillet over medium heat until golden brown, about 2 minutes on each side. Serve immediately.

> **~ COOK'S TIP ~**
>
> Well aged sharp cheddar cheese works best in combination with the strong flavors of the chutney and garlic.

# Tuna and Sun-Dried Tomato Sandwiches

**SERVES 4**

2 7-ounce cans tuna fish, drained

2 tablespoons finely chopped black olives, preferably Kalamata

¼ cup finely chopped drained sun-dried tomatoes packed in oil

3 scallions, finely chopped

4 round Italian or French bread rolls, split open

1 cup arugula or small lettuce leaves

**FOR THE DRESSING**

1½ tablespoons red wine vinegar

5 tablespoons olive oil

¼ cup chopped fresh basil

salt and pepper

**1 ▼** For the dressing, combine the vinegar and oil in a mixing bowl. Whisk until an emulsion is formed. Stir in the basil. Season with salt and pepper.

**2** Add the tuna, olives, sun-dried tomatoes, and scallions and stir.

**3 ▲** Divide the tuna mixture among the rolls. Top with the arugula or lettuce leaves and replace the tops of the rolls, pressing them on firmly.

*Grilled Cheddar and Chutney Sandwiches (top), Tuna and Sun-Dried Tomato Sandwiches*

# Roast Beef Sandwiches with Horseradish Sauce

**SERVES 4**

4 slices of pumpernickel bread

¾ pound roast beef, thinly sliced

salt and pepper

⅓ cup mayonnaise

1½ tablespoons prepared horseradish

2 small tomatoes, seeded and chopped

2 kosher dill pickle spears, chopped

fresh dill sprigs, for garnishing

**1 ▲** Lay the slices of pumpernickel on a flat surface. Divide the slices of roast beef among the pumpernickel, folding the slices in half, if large. Season with salt and pepper.

**2** In a small bowl, combine the mayonnaise and horseradish. Stir in the tomatoes and dill pickle.

**3 ▲** Spoon the horseradish mayonnaise onto the beef. Garnish with dill sprigs and serve.

# Roast Pork and Coleslaw Sandwiches

**SERVES 6**

¾ cup mayonnaise

2 tablespoons ketchup

¼–½ teaspoon cayenne

1 tablespoon light brown sugar

1 pound roast pork, thinly sliced

1 pound green or white cabbage, cut in wedges

2 carrots, finely shredded

1 small green bell pepper, seeded and diced

½ small red onion, finely chopped

12 small round Italian or French bread rolls, split open

~ **VARIATIONS** ~

Instead of roast pork, substitute cooked ham or turkey, and prepare as above. For a change of pace, try tuna in place of meat.

**1 ▲** In a bowl, combine the mayonnaise, ketchup, cayenne, and brown sugar. Stir well.

**2** Stack the slices of roast pork. With a sharp knife, cut them into matchstick strips.

**3** Remove the cores from the cabbage wedges. Lay them on a chopping board and cut into fine strips across the leaves.

**4 ▲** Add the pork, cabbage, carrots, green bell pepper, and red onion to the mayonnaise mixture. Toss to mix.

**5 ▲** Fill the split bread rolls with the pork coleslaw.

*Roast Beef Sandwiches with Horseradish Sauce (top), Roast Pork and Coleslaw Sandwiches*

# Baby Baked Potatoes with Blue Cheese Topping

**MAKES 20**

20 small new potatoes

¼ cup vegetable oil

coarse salt

½ cup sour cream

¼ cup crumbled blue cheese

2 tablespoons chopped fresh chives

**1** Preheat the oven to 350°F.

**2** Wash and dry the potatoes. Pour the oil into a bowl. Add the potatoes and toss to coat well with oil.

**3 ▼** Dip the potatoes in the coarse salt to coat lightly. Spread out the potatoes on a baking sheet. Bake until tender, 45–50 minutes.

**4 ▲** In a small bowl, combine the sour cream and blue cheese.

**5 ▲** Cut a cross in the top of each potato. Press with your fingers to open the potatoes.

**6 ▲** Top each potato with a dollop of the cheese mixture. Sprinkle with chives and serve immediately.

# Guacamole with Cumin Tortilla Chips

**SERVES 10**

2 very ripe avocados

2 shallots or scallions, chopped

2 tablespoons fresh lime juice

1 teaspoon salt

2 teaspoons chili powder

1 medium-size tomato, seeded and chopped

FOR THE CUMIN TORTILLA CHIPS

3 tablespoons corn oil

1½ teaspoons ground cumin

1 teaspoon salt

9 6-inch corn tortillas, each cut in 6 triangles

**1** Preheat the oven to 300°F.

**2 ▲** For the tortilla chips, combine the oil, cumin, and salt in a bowl.

**3 ▲** Spread the tortilla triangles on 2 baking sheets. Brush the seasoned oil on both sides. Bake until they are crisp and golden, about 20 minutes, turning once or twice and brushing with the seasoned oil. Let cool.

**4 ▼** Peel the avocados, discard the pits, and chop the flesh. In a food processor or blender, combine the avocados, shallots or scallions, lime juice, salt, and chili powder. Process until smooth.

**5 ▲** Transfer the mixture to a bowl. Gently stir in the chopped tomato.

**6** Serve the guacamole in a bowl in the center of a platter, surrounded with the cumin tortilla chips.

# Buckwheat Blinis with Marinated Salmon

**MAKES 25**

½ pound salmon fillet, skinned

juice of 1 lime

¼ cup extra-virgin olive oil

pinch salt

3 tablespoons chopped fresh dill

⅔ cup sour cream

¼ avocado, peeled and diced

3 tablespoons chopped fresh chives

fresh dill sprigs, for garnishing

FOR THE BLINIS

¾ cup buckwheat flour

2 teaspoons sugar

1 egg

½ cup milk

2 tablespoons butter or margarine, melted

½ teaspoon cream of tartar

¼ teaspoon baking soda

1 tablespoon water

**1 ▲** With a long, sharp knife, slice the salmon as thinly as possible. Place the slices, in one layer, in a large non-metallic dish.

~ **COOK'S TIP** ~

For easy entertaining, make the blinis early in the day and store, covered. To serve, arrange the blinis on a baking sheet, and reheat in a preheated 400°F oven until hot, about 3–4 minutes.

**2 ▲** In a small bowl, combine the lime juice, olive oil, salt, and chopped dill. Pour the mixture over the salmon. Cover tightly and refrigerate several hours or overnight.

**3 ▲** For the blinis, combine the buckwheat flour and sugar in a mixing bowl. Set aside.

**4 ▲** In a small bowl, beat together the egg, milk, and butter or margarine. Gradually stir the egg mixture into the flour mixture. Stir in the cream of tartar, baking soda, and water.

**5 ▲** Cover the bowl and let the batter stand 1 hour.

**6** With a sharp knife, cut the marinated salmon in thin strips.

**7 ▲** To cook the blinis, heat a heavy nonstick skillet. Using a small ladle or large spoon, drop the batter into the skillet to make small pancakes about 2 inches in diameter. When bubbles appear on the surface, turn over. Cook until the other side is golden brown, 1–2 minutes longer. Transfer the blinis to a plate and continue until all the batter is used.

**8 ▲** To serve, place a teaspoon of sour cream on each blini and top with marinated salmon. Sprinkle with diced avocado and chopped chives and garnish with dill sprigs.

# Cornmeal and Smoked Salmon Muffins

**MAKES 25**

½ cup cornmeal

¼ cup flour

½ teaspoon baking powder

⅛ teaspoon salt

1 tablespoon sugar

1 egg

½ cup buttermilk

¼ cup light cream

½ cup smoked salmon, cut in fine strips

**1** Preheat the oven to 400°F. Grease a mini-muffin tray.

**2** In a mixing bowl, combine the cornmeal, flour, baking powder, salt, and sugar. Set aside.

**3** ▼ In another bowl, mix together the egg, buttermilk, and cream. Gradually add the egg mixture to the cornmeal mixture, stirring quickly until just combined.

**4** ▲ Stir the smoked salmon strips into the batter.

**5** Fill the mini-muffin pans three-quarters full with the batter. Bake until slightly risen and golden brown, 18–20 minutes. Let cool 5 minutes in the pans on a wire rack before unmolding.

# Black Bean and Tomato Salsa in Corncups

**MAKES 30**

1 15-ounce can black (turtle) beans, rinsed and drained

2 tomatoes, seeded and diced

1 garlic clove, minced

1 shallot, minced

1 jalapeño pepper, seeded and chopped

1 teaspoon finely grated lime rind

1 tablespoon olive oil

2 tablespoons fresh lime juice

2 teaspoons maple syrup

salt and pepper

3 tablespoons chopped fresh coriander (cilantro)

FOR THE CORNCUPS

10 6-inch corn tortillas

3–4 tablespoons corn oil, for brushing

**1** Preheat the oven to 400°F.

**2** ▼ For the corncups, using a 2-inch round cookie cutter, cut 3 rounds from each tortilla, pressing firmly to cut through. Discard the tortilla trimmings. Brush both sides of each tortilla round with oil.

**3** Press the tortilla rounds into the cups of 2–3 mini-muffin trays. Bake until the corncups are crisp, about 6 minutes. Let cool on a wire rack.

**4** ▲ In a mixing bowl, combine the beans, tomatoes, garlic, shallot, jalapeño, lime rind, oil, lime juice, and maple syrup. Stir in salt and pepper to taste.

**5** Place a spoonful of the bean and tomato salsa in each corncup. Sprinkle with the chopped coriander just before serving.

*Cornmeal and Smoked Salmon Muffins (top), Black Bean and Tomato Salsa in Corncups*

# Cheese Twists with Cranberry Sauce

**MAKES 12**

6 large sheets of phyllo pastry

½ cup (1 stick) butter or margarine, melted

½ pound Brie cheese, finely diced (rind removed, if wished)

FOR THE SAUCE

1 cup cranberries

2 tablespoons light brown sugar

**1** For the sauce, combine the cranberries and sugar in a small saucepan with just enough water to cover. Bring to a boil and simmer until the cranberries "pop", about 3 minutes, stirring.

**2** ▼ Pour the cranberry mixture into a blender or food processor and process until finely chopped. Press it through a fine-mesh nylon strainer into a bowl. Taste and add more sugar if needed. Set aside.

**3** Preheat the oven to 450°F.

**4** ▲ To make the cheese parcels, cut the phyllo pastry into 36 pieces 5-inches square. Lay one pastry square on a flat surface and brush with some of the butter or margarine. Lay a second pastry square on top, placing it so the corners are not on top of each other. Brush with butter. Lay a third pastry square on top, again placing it so the corners are not on top of the others, thus forming a 12-pointed star.

**5** Put a heaping tablespoon of the diced cheese in the center of each pastry star.

**6** ▲ Bring the points of each pastry star up over the cheese and twist to close securely. Fold back the tips of the points.

**7** Arrange the packages on a baking sheet. Bake until the pastry is crisp and golden brown, 10–15 minutes.

**8** Meanwhile, gently reheat the cranberry sauce. Serve the cheese twists hot with the sauce.

# Bean Nachos

**SERVES 8**

2 tablespoons corn oil

2 onions, chopped

2 garlic cloves, chopped

3 jalapeño peppers, seeded and chopped

1½ tablespoons mild chili powder

1 16-ounce can red kidney beans, drained and liquid reserved

3 tablespoons chopped fresh coriander (cilantro)

nacho chips (fried tortilla rounds) or tortilla chips, for serving

2 cups shredded cheddar cheese

½ cup pitted black olives, thinly sliced

fresh coriander (cilantro) sprigs, for garnishing

**1**  Preheat the oven to 425°F.

**2** ▼  Heat the oil in a skillet. Add the onions, garlic, and jalapeños and cook until soft, about 5 minutes. Add the chili powder and cook 1 minute more.

~ VARIATION ~

To serve as a bean dip, stir in the cheese and olives. Transfer the bean mixture to a round earthenware dish. Bake until the cheese melts and browns slightly, 10–15 minutes. Garnish with coriander, and serve with tortilla chips for dipping.

**3** ▲  Stir the beans into the onion mixture with ½ cup of the reserved can liquid. Cook until thickened, about 10 minutes, mashing the beans with a fork from time to time. Remove the pan from the heat and stir in the chopped coriander.

**4** ▼  Put a little of the bean mixture on each nacho chip. Top each nacho with a little cheese and a slice of olive. Arrange on a baking sheet.

**5**  Bake until the cheese has melted and is beginning to brown, 5–10 minutes. Serve immediately. Garnish with coriander, if liked.

# Spinach and Feta Phyllo Triangles

**SERVES 20**

2 tablespoons olive oil

2 shallots, finely chopped

1 pound frozen spinach, thawed

¼ pound feta cheese, crumbled

⅓ cup walnut pieces, chopped

¼ teaspoon grated nutmeg

salt and pepper

4 large or 8 small sheets phyllo pastry

½ cup (1 stick) butter or margarine, melted

1  Preheat the oven to 400°F.

**2** ▲  Heat the olive oil in a skillet. Add the shallots and cook until softened, about 5 minutes.

**3** ▲  A handful at a time, squeeze all the liquid out of the spinach. Add the spinach to the shallots. Increase the heat to high and cook, stirring, until all excess moisture has evaporated, about 5 minutes.

**4** ▲  Transfer the spinach mixture to a bowl. Let cool. Stir in the feta and walnuts. Season with nutmeg, salt and pepper.

**5** ▲  Lay a phyllo sheet on a flat surface. (Keep the remaining phyllo covered with a damp cloth to prevent it drying out.) Brush with some of the butter or margarine. Lay a second phyllo sheet on top of the first. With scissors, cut the layered phyllo pastry lengthwise into 3-inch-wide strips.

~ **VARIATION** ~

For an alternative filling, omit the spinach and shallots. Use ¾ pound goat cheese, crumbled, instead of the feta cheese, and ½ cup toasted pine nuts instead of the walnuts. Mix the cheese with the olive oil and 1 tablespoon chopped fresh basil. Assemble as above.

**6** ▲  Place a tablespoonful of the spinach mixture at the end of one strip of phyllo pastry.

**7** ▲  Fold a bottom corner of the pastry over the filling to form a triangle, then continue folding over the pastry strip to the other end. Fill and shape the triangles until all the ingredients are used.

**8** ▲  Set the triangles on baking sheets and brush with butter. Bake the phyllo triangles until they are crispy and golden brown, about 10 minutes. Serve hot.

# Potato Pancakes with Lemon-Chive Cream

**MAKES 40**

2 tablespoons butter or margarine

1 shallot, finely chopped

1 egg

½ pound potatoes

oil for frying

FOR THE LEMON-CHIVE CREAM

½ cup cream cheese, at room temperature

2 tablespoons sour cream

1 teaspoon finely grated lemon rind

1 tablespoon fresh lemon juice

1 tablespoon chopped fresh chives

**1** Melt the butter or margarine in a small skillet. Add the shallot and cook until softened, about 3 minutes. Set aside and let cool.

**2** Beat the egg in a large mixing bowl until light and frothy.

**3** Coarsely grate the potatoes. Add them to the bowl and mix with the egg until completely coated. Season generously with salt and pepper. Add the shallot and mix well.

**4** ▼ For the lemon-chive cream, combine the cream cheese and sour cream in a bowl. Beat until smooth. Add the lemon rind and juice and chives. Set aside.

**5** ▲ Heat ¼ inch of oil in a skillet. Drop teaspoonfuls of the potato mixture into the hot oil and press them with the back of a spoon to make flat rounds. Fry until well browned, 2–3 minutes on each side. Drain on paper towels and keep warm while frying the remaining pancakes.

**6** Serve the pancakes hot, with the lemon-chive cream for spooning on top, or for dipping.

---

# Crab-Stuffed Cherry Tomatoes

**MAKES 40**

¼ pound lump crab meat

1 teaspoon chili sauce

¼ teaspoon Dijon-style mustard

2 tablespoons mayonnaise

½ teaspoon Worcestershire sauce

2 scallions, finely chopped

1 tablespoon chopped fresh basil

1 tablespoon chopped fresh chives

40 cherry tomatoes

salt

**1** In a mixing bowl, combine the crab meat, chili sauce, mustard, mayonnaise, Worcestershire sauce, scallions, and herbs. Mix well. Cover and refrigerate until needed.

**2** ▲ Using a serrated knife, cut a very thin slice from the stem end of each tomato. Carefully scoop out the pulp and seeds with the tip of a teaspoon.

**3** Sprinkle the insides of the tomato shells lightly with salt. Invert them on paper towels and let them drain 15 minutes.

**4** ▲ Using a small spoon, stuff the tomatoes with the crab, mounding the filling slightly on top. Serve cold.

*Potato Pancakes with Lemon-Chive Cream (top), Crab-Stuffed Cherry Tomatoes*

# FISH & SEAFOOD

~

*Whether fresh from the sea, or frozen or canned, fish and
seafood make nutritious and easy-to-prepare dishes. The
recipes here offer exciting ideas, from rich casseroles and
chowders to tasty kabobs and broiled steaks.*

# Swordfish with Orange-Caper Sauce

**SERVES 4**

¼ cup fresh orange juice

1 teaspoon soy sauce

2 tablespoons olive oil

4 swordfish steaks (about ½ pound each)

salt and pepper

3 tablespoons cold butter or margarine, cut in pieces

2 tablespoons capers in vinegar

1 tablespoon chopped fresh parsley

**1** In a small bowl, combine the orange juice, soy sauce, and 1 tablespoon of the olive oil. Whisk to mix.

**2** Lay the swordfish steaks in a shallow baking dish. Pour the orange-soy mixture over them and sprinkle with salt and pepper.

**3** Heat the remaining tablespoon of olive oil in a heavy skillet over medium-high heat.

**4** ▲ Drain the swordfish steaks, reserving the marinade. Add the steaks to the skillet and cook until the fish flakes easily when tested with a fork, 3–4 minutes on each side, basting occasionally with the reserved marinade. Transfer the swordfish steaks to a warmed serving platter.

**5** ▲ Pour the reserved marinade into the skillet and cook 1 minute, stirring to mix in the cooking juices. Add the butter or margarine, capers with their vinegar, and parsley. Cook until the butter has melted and the sauce is slightly syrupy.

**6** Pour the sauce over the swordfish steaks and serve immediately.

---

# Tuna Steaks with Ginger-Soy Vinaigrette

**SERVES 6**

6 tuna steaks (about 2 pounds)

FOR THE VINAIGRETTE

1-inch piece of fresh gingerroot, peeled and finely grated

2 scallions, thinly sliced

2 tablespoons chopped fresh chives

grated rind and juice of 1 lime

2 tablespoons dry sherry wine

1 tablespoon soy sauce

½ cup olive oil

salt and pepper

**1** ▲ For the vinaigrette, combine the gingerroot, scallions, chives, lime rind and juice, sherry, and soy sauce. Add the olive oil and whisk to mix. Season with salt and pepper. Set aside.

**2** Preheat the broiler. Sprinkle the tuna steaks with salt and pepper.

**3** ▼ Arrange the tuna steaks on the rack in the broiler pan. Broil about 3 inches from the heat for about 5 minutes on each side, until the fish flakes easily when tested with a fork.

**4** Arrange the cooked fish on a warmed serving platter or individual plates. Spoon the ginger vinaigrette over the fish, and serve.

*Swordfish with Orange-Caper Sauce (top), Tuna Steaks with Ginger-Soy Vinaigrette*

# Cornmeal-Coated Cod with Tomato Sauce

**SERVES 4**

3 tablespoons cornmeal

½ teaspoon salt

¼ teaspoon hot chili powder or cayenne

4 cod steaks, each 1-inch thick (about 1½ pounds)

2 tablespoons corn oil

fresh basil sprigs, for garnishing

FOR THE TOMATO SAUCE

2 tablespoons olive oil

1 shallot or ½ small onion, finely chopped

1 garlic clove, minced

1 pound ripe tomatoes, chopped, or 1 16-ounce can crushed tomatoes

⅛ teaspoon sugar

¼ cup dry white wine

2 tablespoons chopped fresh basil or ½ teaspoon dried basil

salt and pepper

**1** For the sauce, heat the oil in a saucepan. Add the shallot or onion and the garlic and cook until soft, about 5 minutes. Stir in the tomatoes, sugar, wine, and basil. Bring to a boil. Simmer until thickened, 10–15 minutes.

**2** ▲ Work the sauce through a vegetable mill or strainer until smooth. Return it to the pan. Season with salt and pepper. Set aside.

**3** ▲ Combine the cornmeal, salt, and chili powder or cayenne on a sheet of wax paper.

**4** ▲ Rinse the cod steaks, then dip them on both sides into the cornmeal mixture, patting gently to make an even coating.

**5** ▲ Heat the corn oil in a large frying pan. Add the cod steaks and cook until golden brown and the flesh will flake easily when tested with a fork, about 5 minutes on each side. Cook in batches if necessary. Meanwhile, reheat the tomato sauce.

**6** Garnish the cod steaks with basil sprigs and serve with the tomato sauce.

# Cajun Blackened Swordfish

**SERVES 4**

| |
|---|
| 1 teaspoon onion powder |
| 1 teaspoon garlic salt |
| 2 teaspoons paprika |
| 1 teaspoon ground cumin |
| 1 teaspoon mustard powder |
| 1 teaspoon cayenne |
| 2 teaspoons dried thyme |
| 2 teaspoons dried oregano |
| ½ teaspoon salt |
| 1 teaspoon pepper |
| 4 swordfish steaks (about 1½ pounds) |
| 4 tablespoons butter or margarine, melted |
| dill sprigs, for garnishing |

**1** In a small bowl, combine all the spices, herbs, and seasonings.

**2** ▲ Brush both sides of the fish steaks with some of the melted butter or margarine.

**3** ▲ Coat both sides of the fish steaks with the seasoning mixture, rubbing it in well.

**4** Heat a large heavy skillet until a drop of water sprinkled on the surface sizzles, about 5 minutes.

**5** ▲ Drizzle 2 teaspoons of the remaining butter or margarine over the fish steaks. Add the steaks to the skillet, butter-side down, and cook until the underside is blackened, 2–3 minutes.

**6** ▲ Drizzle another 2 teaspoons melted butter or margarine over the fish, then turn the steaks over. Cook until the second side is blackened and the fish flakes easily when tested with a fork, 2–3 minutes more.

**7** Transfer the fish to warmed plates, garnish with dill, and drizzle with the remaining butter or margarine.

# Salmon Steaks with Lime Butter

**SERVES 4**

4 salmon steaks (about 1½ pounds)

salt and pepper

FOR THE LIME BUTTER

4 tablespoons butter or margarine, at room temperature

1 tablespoon chopped fresh coriander (cilantro), or 1 teaspoon dried coriander

1 teaspoon finely grated lime rind

1 tablespoon fresh lime juice

**1** For the lime butter, combine the butter or margarine, coriander, and lime rind and juice in a bowl. Mix well with a fork.

**2 ▲** Transfer the lime butter to a piece of wax paper and shape into a log. Roll in the paper until smooth and round. Refrigerate until firm, about 1 hour.

**3** Preheat the broiler.

**4 ▼** Sprinkle the salmon steaks with salt and pepper. Arrange them on the rack in the broiler pan. Broil about 3 inches from the heat, 5 minutes on each side.

**5** Unwrap the lime butter and cut into 4 pieces. Top each salmon steak with a pat of lime butter and serve.

# Citrus Fish Fillets

**SERVES 6**

1–2 tablespoons butter or margarine, melted

2 pounds sole fillets

salt and pepper

1 teaspoon grated lemon rind

1 teaspoon grated orange rind

2 tablespoons fresh orange juice

⅓ cup whipping cream

1 tablespoon chopped fresh basil

fresh basil sprigs, for garnishing

**1** Preheat the oven to 350°F. Generously grease a large baking dish with the melted butter or margarine.

~ **VARIATION** ~

Use an equal amount of grapefruit rind and juice to replace the lemon and orange.

**2 ▲** Lay the fish fillets skin-side down in the baking dish, in one layer. Sprinkle with salt and pepper.

**3 ▲** In a small bowl, combine the lemon and orange rinds and orange juice. Pour the mixture over the fish.

**4** Bake until the fish flakes easily when tested with a fork, 15–20 minutes. Transfer the fish to a warmed serving platter.

**5 ▲** Strain the juices from the baking dish into a small saucepan. Stir in the cream and chopped basil. Boil until thickened, about 5 minutes.

**6** Spoon the citrus cream over the fish fillets. Garnish with basil sprigs and serve.

*Salmon Steaks with Lime Butter (top), Citrus Fish Fillets*

# Sweet and Spicy Salmon Fillets

**SERVES 6**

2 pounds salmon fillet, cut in 6 pieces

½ cup honey

¼ cup soy sauce

juice of 1 lime

1 tablespoon sesame oil

¼ teaspoon hot red pepper flakes

¼ teaspoon crushed black peppercorns

~ COOK'S TIP ~

The acid in the citrus juice begins to "cook" the fish, so broiling on one side only is sufficient.

1  Place the salmon pieces skin-side down in a large baking dish, in one layer.

2 ▲  In a bowl, combine the honey, soy sauce, lime juice, sesame oil, pepper flakes, and peppercorns.

3 ▲  Pour the mixture over the fish. Cover and let marinate 30 minutes.

4  Preheat the broiler. Remove the fish from the marinade and arrange on the rack in the broiler pan, skin-side down. Broil about 3 inches from the heat until the fish flakes easily when tested with a fork, 6–8 minutes.

# Peppercorn-Crusted Cod Steaks

**SERVES 4**

1 teaspoon each pink, white, and green peppercorns

3 tablespoons butter or margarine

4 cod steaks, each 1-inch thick (about 1 pound)

salt

½ cup fish stock or bottled clam juice

½ cup whipping cream

¼ cup chopped fresh chives

1 ▼  Wrap the peppercorns in a dish towel or heavy plastic bag and crush with a rolling pin.

2  Melt the butter or margarine in a large frying pan. Remove from the heat. Brush the cod steaks with some of the butter or margarine.

3 ▲  Press the crushed peppercorns onto both sides of the cod steaks. Season with salt.

4  Heat the frying pan. Add the cod steaks and cook over medium-low heat until the fish flakes easily when tested with a fork, about 4 minutes on each side. Transfer the steaks to a warmed serving platter.

5 ▲  Add the stock or clam juice and cream to the frying pan and bring to a boil, stirring well. Boil until reduced by half, about 5 minutes. Remove from the heat and stir in the chives.

6  Pour the sauce over the fish and serve immediately.

~ VARIATION ~

In place of cod, use monkfish, cut into steaks or thick fillets. The flavor is similar to lobster.

*Sweet and Spicy Salmon Fillets (top), Peppercorn-Crusted Cod Steaks*

# Breaded Fish with Tartare Sauce

SERVES 4

½ cup dry bread crumbs

1 teaspoon dried oregano

½ teaspoon cayenne

1 cup milk

2 teaspoons salt

4 pieces of cod fillet (about 1½ pounds)

3 tablespoons butter or margarine, melted

FOR THE TARTARE SAUCE

½ cup mayonnaise

½ teaspoon Dijon-style mustard

1 kosher dill pickle spear, finely chopped

1 tablespoon drained capers, chopped

1 teaspoon chopped fresh parsley

1 teaspoon chopped fresh chives

1 teaspoon chopped fresh tarragon

salt and pepper

**1** Preheat the oven to 450°F. Grease a shallow glass or porcelain baking dish.

**2** ▲ Combine the bread crumbs, oregano, and cayenne on a plate and blend together. Mix the milk with the salt in a bowl, stirring well to dissolve the salt.

**3** ▲ Dip the pieces of cod fillet in the milk, then transfer to the plate and coat with the bread crumb mixture.

**4** ▲ Arrange the coated fish in the prepared baking dish, in one layer. Drizzle the melted butter or margarine over the fish.

**5** Bake until the fish flakes easily when tested with a fork, 10–15 minutes.

**6** ▲ Meanwhile, for the tartare sauce, combine all the ingredients in a small bowl. Stir gently to mix well.

**7** Serve the fish hot, accompanied by the tartare sauce.

# Stuffed Sole Rolls

**SERVES 4**

8 skinless sole fillets (about 1 pound)

1 tablespoon butter or margarine, cut in 8 pieces

¼ cup dry white wine

paprika, for garnishing

FOR THE STUFFING

2 tablespoons butter or margarine

1 small onion, finely chopped

1 handful of fresh spinach leaves, shredded (1 cup firmly packed)

2 tablespoons pine nuts, toasted

2 tablespoons raisins

2 tablespoons fresh bread crumbs

⅛ teaspoon ground cinnamon

salt and pepper

**1** Preheat the oven to 400°F. Butter a shallow baking dish.

**2 ▲** For the stuffing, melt the butter or margarine in a small saucepan. Add the onion and cook over medium heat until softened, about 5 minutes. Stir in the spinach and cook, stirring constantly, until the spinach wilts and renders its liquid.

**3** Add the pine nuts, raisins, bread crumbs, cinnamon, and a little salt and pepper. Raise the heat and cook until most of the liquid has evaporated, stirring constantly. Remove from the heat.

**4 ▲** Sprinkle the sole fillets with salt and pepper. Place a spoonful of the spinach stuffing at one end of each fillet. Roll up and secure with a wooden toothpick, if necessary.

**5 ▲** Place the sole rolls in the prepared baking dish. Put a small piece of butter or margarine on each roll. Pour the wine over the fish. Cover the baking dish with foil and bake until the fish flakes easily when tested with a fork, about 15 minutes.

**6** Serve on warmed plates with a little of the cooking juices spooned over the fish.

~ **VARIATION** ~

Instead of sole, other lean fish fillets may be used, such as flounder, whitefish, perch, or orange roughy.

# Red Snapper Veracruz

**SERVES 4**

3 tablespoons flour

salt and pepper

1½ pounds red snapper fillets or other firm white-fish fillets

1 tablespoon butter or margarine

2 tablespoons olive oil

1 onion, sliced

2 garlic cloves, chopped

¼ teaspoon ground cumin

1½ cups peeled, seeded, and chopped fresh tomatoes or canned crushed tomatoes

½ cup fresh orange juice

orange wedges, for garnishing

**1 ▼** Put the flour on a plate and season with salt and pepper. Coat the fish fillets lightly with the seasoned flour, shaking off any excess.

**2** Heat the butter or margarine and half the oil in a large skillet. Add the fish fillets to the skillet and cook until golden brown and the flesh flakes easily when tested with a fork, about 3 minutes on each side.

**3 ▲** When the fish is cooked, transfer to a heated serving platter. Cover with foil and keep warm while making the sauce.

**4 ▲** Heat the remaining oil in the skillet. Add the onion and garlic and cook until softened, about 5 minutes.

**5 ▲** Stir in the cumin, tomatoes, and orange juice. Bring to a boil and cook until thickened, about 10 minutes, stirring frequently.

**6** Garnish the fish with orange wedges. Pass the sauce separately.

# Baked Stuffed Trout

**SERVES 4**

| |
|---|
| 2 tablespoons butter or margarine |
| 1 onion, chopped |
| 1 celery stalk, diced |
| 1 cup fresh bread cubes |
| 1 tablespoon fresh thyme leaves or 1 teaspoon dried thyme |
| salt and pepper |
| 4 trout, dressed (about ½ pound each) |
| 8 bacon slices |
| celery leaves or parsley, for garnishing |

**1** Preheat the oven to 450°F.

**2** ▲ Melt the butter or margarine in a frying pan. Add the onion and celery and cook until softened, about 5 minutes. Remove the pan from the heat. Add the bread cubes, thyme, and season with salt and pepper to taste. Stir to mix well.

**3** ▲ Season the cavity of each trout with salt and pepper.

**4** ▲ Stuff each trout with the bread mixture, dividing it evenly among the fish. If necessary, secure the openings with wooden toothpicks.

**5** ▼ Wrap 2 bacon slices around each stuffed trout. Arrange in a baking dish, in one layer.

**6** Bake until the fish flakes easily when tested with a fork and the bacon is crisp, 35–40 minutes. Serve garnished with celery leaves or sprigs of parsley.

# Halibut with Lemon-Pineapple Relish

**SERVES 4**

4 halibut steaks (about 1½ pounds)

2 tablespoons butter or margarine, melted

salt and pepper

fresh mint sprigs, for garnishing

FOR THE RELISH

½ cup finely diced fresh pineapple

2 tablespoons diced red bell pepper

1 tablespoon minced red onion

finely grated rind of 1 lemon

1 tablespoon lemon juice

1 teaspoon honey

2 tablespoons chopped fresh mint

**1** For the relish, combine the pineapple, bell pepper, red onion, lemon rind and juice, and honey in a small bowl. Stir to mix. Cover with plastic wrap and refrigerate 30 minutes.

**2** Preheat the broiler.

**3** ▲ Brush the halibut with butter or margarine and sprinkle with salt and pepper. Arrange on the rack in the broiler pan, buttered-side up.

**4** Broil the steaks about 3 inches from the heat, turning once and brushing with the remaining butter or margarine, about 5 minutes on each side. Transfer to warmed serving plates.

**5** ▲ Stir the chopped mint into the pineapple relish. Garnish the halibut with mint sprigs and serve with the relish.

# Fish Chowder

**SERVES 4**

3 thick-cut bacon slices, cut in small pieces

1 large onion, chopped

2 large potatoes, cut in ¾-inch cubes (about 1½ pounds)

salt and pepper

4 cups fish stock or bottled clam juice

1 pound skinless haddock or cod fillet, cut in 1-inch cubes

2 tablespoons chopped fresh parsley

1 tablespoon chopped fresh chives

1 cup whipping cream or whole milk

**1** Fry the bacon in a deep saucepan until the fat is rendered. Add the onion and potatoes and cook over low heat, without browning, about 10 minutes. Season to taste with salt and pepper.

**2** ▲ Pour off excess bacon fat from the pan. Add the fish stock to the pan and bring to a boil. Simmer until the vegetables are tender, 15–20 minutes.

**3** ▲ Stir in the cubes of fish, the parsley, and chives. Simmer until the fish is just cooked, 3–4 minutes.

**4** Stir the cream or milk into the chowder and reheat gently. Season to taste and serve immediately.

*Halibut with Lemon-Pineapple Relish (top), Fish Chowder*

# Crab Cakes

**SERVES 3 OR 6**

| |
|---|
| 1 pound fresh lump crab meat |
| 1 egg, well beaten |
| 1 teaspoon Dijon-style mustard |
| 2 teaspoons prepared horseradish |
| 2 teaspoons Worcestershire sauce |
| 8 scallions, finely chopped |
| ¼ cup chopped fresh parsley |
| 1½ cups fresh bread crumbs |
| salt and pepper |
| 1 tablespoon whipping cream (optional) |
| ½ cup dry bread crumbs |
| 3 tablespoons butter or margarine |
| lemon wedges, for serving |

**1** In a mixing bowl, combine the crab meat, egg, mustard, horseradish, Worcestershire sauce, scallions, parsley, fresh bread crumbs, and seasoning. Mix gently, leaving the pieces of crab meat as large as possible. If the mixture is too dry to hold together, add the cream.

**2** ▲ Divide the crab mixture into 6 portions and shape each into a patty.

**3** ▲ Put the dry bread crumbs on a plate. Coat the crab cakes on both sides with crumbs.

**4** Melt the butter or margarine in a skillet. Fry the crab cakes until golden, about 3 minutes on each side. Add more fat if necessary.

**5** Serve 1 or 2 per person, with lemon wedges.

---

# Baked Stuffed Crab

**SERVES 4**

| |
|---|
| 4 freshly cooked crabs |
| 1 celery stalk, diced |
| 1 scallion, finely chopped |
| 1 small fresh green chili pepper, seeded and finely chopped |
| ⅓ cup mayonnaise |
| 2 tablespoons fresh lemon juice |
| 1 tablespoon chopped fresh chives |
| salt and pepper |
| ½ cup fresh bread crumbs |
| ½ cup grated Monterey Jack cheese |
| 2 tablespoons butter or margarine, melted |
| parsley sprigs, for garnishing |

**1** Preheat the oven to 375°F.

**2** ▼ Pull the claws and legs from each crab. Separate the body from the shell. Scoop out the meat from the shell. Discard the feathery gills and the intestines; remove the meat and coral from the body. Crack the claws, and remove the meat.

**3** Scrub the shells. Cut into the seam on the underside with scissors. The inner part of the shell should break off cleanly along the seam, enlarging the opening. Rinse the shells and dry them well.

**4** In a bowl, combine the crab meat, celery, scallion, chili pepper, mayonnaise, lemon juice, and chives. Season with salt and pepper to taste and mix well.

**5** In another bowl, toss together the bread crumbs, cheese, and melted butter or margarine.

**6** ▲ Pile the crab mixture into the shells. Sprinkle with the bread-cheese mixture. Bake until golden brown, about 20 minutes. Serve hot, garnished with parsley sprigs.

*Crab Cakes (top), Baked Stuffed Crab*

# Paella

**SERVES 6**

4 tablespoons olive oil

1½ cups short-grain rice

1 large onion, chopped

1 red bell pepper, seeded and chopped

¾ pound squid, cleaned and cut in rings (optional)

2¼ cups fish or chicken stock

½ cup dry white wine

½ teaspoon saffron threads

1 large garlic clove, minced

1 cup canned crushed tomatoes

1 bay leaf

¼ teaspoon finely grated lemon rind

¼ pound chorizo or other spicy cooked sausage, cut across into ¼-inch slices

salt and pepper

1½ cups fresh or frozen green peas

¾ pound monkfish, skinned and cut in 1-inch pieces

24 mussels, well scrubbed

12 raw or cooked jumbo shrimp, peeled and deveined

**1 ▼** Heat the olive oil in a large, wide skillet or paella pan. Add the rice and cook over medium-high heat until it begins to color, stirring frequently.

**2 ▲** Stir in the onion and bell pepper and cook 2–3 minutes longer.

**3 ▲** Add the squid, if using, and cook, stirring occasionally, until it is lightly browned.

**4** Stir in the stock, wine, saffron, and garlic. Bring to a boil.

**5 ▲** Add the tomatoes, bay leaf, lemon rind, and sausage. Season with salt and pepper. Return to a boil, then reduce the heat to low. Cover and simmer until the rice has absorbed most of the liquid, about 15 minutes.

**6 ▲** Add the peas, monkfish, and mussels to the rice. Push the mussels down into the rice.

**7 ▲** Gently stir in the shrimp. Cover and continue cooking until the mussels have opened and the rice is tender, about 5 minutes. Raw shrimp should have turned bright pink.

**8** Taste and adjust the seasoning. Serve immediately in a heated serving dish or from the paella pan, if using.

~ COOK'S TIP ~

This recipe can be doubled to feed a crowd. Be sure to use a larger pan, such as a wide shallow flameproof casserole. The final simmering, after the pan has been covered (step 5), can be done in a preheated 375°F oven. If using a paella pan, cover with foil.

# Seafood and Vegetable Stir-Fry

**SERVES 4**

1 pound rice vermicelli

2 tablespoons oil drained from sun-dried tomatoes

½ cup sun-dried tomatoes packed in oil, drained and sliced

½ cup scallions, cut diagonally in ½-inch pieces

2 large carrots, cut in thin sticks

1 zucchini, cut in thin sticks

½ pound raw shrimp, peeled and deveined

½ pound sea scallops

1-inch piece of fresh gingerroot, peeled and finely grated

3 tablespoons fresh lemon juice

3 tablespoons chopped fresh basil or 1 teaspoon dried basil

salt and pepper

**1** ▲ Bring a large saucepan of water to a boil. Add the rice vermicelli and cook until tender (check package directions for timing). Drain, rinse with boiling water, and drain again thoroughly. Keep warm.

**2** ▲ Heat the oil in a wok over high heat. Add the tomatoes, scallions, and carrots and stir-fry 5 minutes.

**3** ▲ Add the zucchini, shrimp, scallops, and gingerroot. Stir-fry 3 minutes.

**4** ▲ Add the lemon juice, basil, and salt and pepper to taste and stir well. Stir-fry until the shrimp are all pink, about 2 more minutes.

**5** Serve on the rice vermicelli.

# Seafood Stew

**SERVES 6**

3 tablespoons olive oil

2 large onions, chopped

1 small green bell pepper, seeded and sliced

3 carrots, chopped

3 garlic cloves, minced

2 tablespoons tomato paste

2 16-ounce cans crushed tomatoes

¼ cup chopped fresh parsley

1 teaspoon fresh thyme leaves or ¼ teaspoon dried thyme

1 tablespoon chopped fresh basil or 1 teaspoon dried basil

½ cup dry white wine

1 pound raw shrimp, peeled and deveined

3 pounds mussels or clams (in shells), or a mixture of both, thoroughly cleaned

2 pounds halibut fillet, cut in 2- to 3-inch pieces

1½ cups fish stock or water

salt and pepper

extra chopped fresh herbs, for garnishing

**1 ▲** Heat the oil in a flameproof casserole. Add the onions, green bell pepper, carrots, and garlic and cook until tender, about 5 minutes.

**2** Add the tomato paste, canned tomatoes, herbs, and wine and stir well to combine. Bring to a boil and simmer 20 minutes.

**3 ▲** Add the shrimp, mussels, clams, halibut pieces and stock. Season with salt and pepper.

**4 ▲** Bring back to a boil, then reduce the heat and simmer until the shrimp turn pink, the pieces of fish will flake easily, and the mussels and clams open, about 5 minutes.

**5** Serve in large soup plates, garnished with chopped herbs.

# Shrimp Creole

**SERVES 4**

4 tablespoons butter or margarine

3 garlic cloves, minced

1 large onion, finely chopped

1 green bell pepper, seeded and finely chopped

1 cup chopped celery

2 cups canned crushed tomatoes

1 teaspoon sugar

2 teaspoons salt

1 bay leaf

1½ teaspoons fresh thyme leaves or ½ teaspoon dried thyme

¼ teaspoon cayenne

2 pounds raw shrimp, peeled and deveined

½ teaspoon grated lemon rind

2 tablespoons fresh lemon juice

pepper

**1** Heat the butter or margarine in a flameproof casserole. Add the garlic, onion, bell pepper, and celery and cook until softened, about 5 minutes.

**2** ▲ Add the tomatoes, sugar, salt, bay leaf, thyme, and cayenne. Bring to a boil. Reduce the heat and simmer 10 minutes.

**3** ▲ Stir in the shrimp, lemon rind and juice, and pepper to taste. Cover and simmer until the shrimp turn pink, about 5 minutes.

**4** Serve immediately on a bed of freshly cooked rice.

---

# Shrimp in Creamy Mustard Sauce

**SERVES 4**

4 tablespoons butter or margarine

2 pounds raw shrimp, peeled and deveined

2 shallots, finely chopped

4 scallions, cut diagonally in ⅛-inch slices

2 tablespoons fresh lemon juice

½ cup dry white wine

½ cup whipping cream

2 tablespoons whole-grain mustard

salt and pepper

**2** Melt the remaining butter or margarine in the skillet. Add the shallots and scallions and cook until softened, 3–4 minutes, stirring frequently.

**3** ▲ Stir in the lemon juice and wine. Bring to a boil, scraping the bottom of the pan with a wooden spoon to mix in the cooking juices.

**4** ▲ Add the cream. Simmer until the mixture thickens, 3–4 minutes, stirring frequently. Stir in the mustard.

**5** Return the shrimp to the skillet and reheat briefly. Season with salt and pepper and serve.

**1** Melt half the butter or margarine in a skillet over high heat. Add the shrimp and cook until they turn pink and opaque, about 2 minutes, stirring constantly. Remove with a slotted spoon and set aside.

*Shrimp Creole (top), Shrimp in Creamy Mustard Sauce*

# New England Clambake with Lobster

**SERVES 6**

fresh seaweed

salt

6 1-pound lobsters

2 pounds pickling onions, peeled

2 pounds small red potatoes

3 dozen littleneck or cherrystone clams

6 ears of corn, husks and silk removed

1 cup (2 sticks) butter or margarine

3 tablespoons chopped fresh chives

**1** Put a layer of seaweed in the bottom of a deep kettle containing 1 inch of salted water. Put the lobsters on top and cover with more seaweed.

**2** Add the onions and potatoes. Cover the kettle and bring the water to a boil.

**3** ▲ After 10 minutes, add the clams and the ears of corn. Cover again and cook until the clams have opened, the lobster shells are red, and the potatoes are tender, 15–20 minutes longer.

**4** ▲ Meanwhile, in a small saucepan melt the butter or margarine and stir in the chives.

**5** Discard the seaweed. Serve the lobsters and clams with the vegetables, accompanied by the chive butter.

# Scallop Kabobs

**SERVES 4**

16 sea scallops

½ teaspoon ground ginger

1 8-ounce can pineapple chunks in juice, drained and juice reserved

1 small fresh red chili pepper, seeded and chopped

grated rind and juice of 1 lime

16 snow peas

16 cherry tomatoes

8 baby zucchini, halved

**1** Put the scallops in a bowl. Add the ginger, the juice from the pineapple, the chili pepper, and lime rind and juice and stir well. Cover and let marinate at room temperature about 20 minutes, or 2 hours in the refrigerator.

**2** Preheat the broiler.

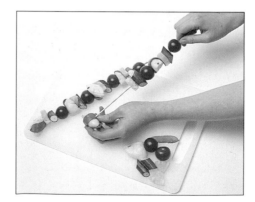

**3** ▲ Drain the scallops, reserving their marinade. Wrap a snow pea around a scallop and thread onto 1 of 4 skewers. Thread on a cherry tomato, a piece of zucchini, and a piece of pineapple, followed by another snow pea-wrapped scallop. Repeat until all the ingredients have been used.

**4** ▲ Lay the kabobs in the broiler pan and brush with the reserved marinade.

**5** Broil about 3 inches from the heat, brushing frequently with the marinade and turning occasionally, until the scallops are opaque, 4–5 minutes.

**6** Serve immediately, on a bed of cooked rice, if wished.

*New England Clambake with Lobster (top), Scallop Kabobs*

# MEAT & POULTRY

~

*For most people, meat and poultry are the heart of a good meal, so new and interesting recipes for beef, lamb, pork, chicken, and turkey are always welcome. Here are lots of good ideas, from snacks to barbecue fare, and stews to roasts.*

# Layered Meat Loaf with Fruit

**SERVES 6**

1½ pounds ground chuck

½ pound ground pork

2 eggs, lightly beaten

1 cup fresh bread crumbs

¼ teaspoon ground cinnamon

salt and pepper

FOR THE STUFFING

1 tablespoon butter or margarine

1 small onion, chopped

¼ cup chopped dried figs

¼ cup chopped dried apricots

¼ cup golden raisins

¼ cup pine nuts

½ cup dry white wine

2 tablespoons chopped fresh parsley

1  Preheat the oven to 350°F.

2 ▼  For the stuffing, melt the butter or margarine in a small frying pan. Add the onion and cook until softened, about 5 minutes. Stir in the figs, apricots, raisins, pine nuts and wine. Bring to a boil and boil to evaporate the liquid, about 5 minutes. Remove from the heat and stir in the parsley. Set aside.

3  In a bowl, mix together the beef, pork, eggs, bread crumbs, cinnamon, and a little salt and pepper.

4 ▲  Press half of the meat mixture over the bottom of a 9- × 5-inch loaf pan. Spoon the stuffing mixture over the meat. Spread the remaining meat mixture on top and press down gently.

5  Cover the pan with foil. Bake 1¼ hours. Pour off any excess fat from the pan. Let the meat loaf cool slightly before serving.

# Steak with Spicy Mushroom Sauce

**SERVES 4**

5 tablespoons butter or margarine

1 pound mushrooms, quartered

1 shallot, finely chopped

¼ cup chopped fresh parsley

salt and pepper

4 beef top loin or rib eye steaks, each about 1-inch thick

1 onion, thinly sliced

⅛ teaspoon hot red pepper flakes

⅛ teaspoon cayenne

dash of hot pepper sauce

2 teaspoons Worcestershire sauce

2 teaspoons sugar

⅔ cup brandy

1 cup beef stock

1 ▼  Melt 2 tablespoons of the butter or margarine in a frying pan. Add the mushrooms and shallot, and cook until softened, about 5 minutes. Drain off the excess liquid. Sprinkle the mushrooms with the parsley and a little salt and pepper. Set aside.

2  Preheat the broiler. Sprinkle the steaks with salt and pepper and arrange them on the rack in the broiler pan. Set aside.

3  Melt the remaining butter or margarine in a saucepan. Add the onion and cook until softened, about 5 minutes. Stir in the red pepper flakes, cayenne, hot pepper sauce, Worcestershire sauce, sugar, and brandy. Bring to a boil and boil until the sauce is reduced by half.

4  Meanwhile, broil the steaks about 3 inches from the heat, 5 minutes on each side for medium-rare, 8 minutes on each side for medium.

5  While the steaks are cooking, add the stock to the sauce and boil again to reduce by half. Season to taste with salt and pepper. Stir in the cooked mushrooms.

6  Transfer the steaks to heated plates and spoon the sauce on top.

*Layered Meat Loaf with Fruit (top), Steak with Spicy Mushroom Sauce*

# Guacamole Cheeseburgers

**SERVES 6**

2 pounds ground chuck

salt and pepper

6 slices of Swiss cheese

6 hamburger buns with sesame seeds,
   split and toasted

2 large tomatoes, sliced

FOR THE GUACAMOLE

1 large ripe avocado

1 scallion, chopped

2 teaspoons fresh lemon juice

1 teaspoon chili powder

2 tablespoons chopped fresh tomato

**1** To make the guacamole, peel the
avocado, discard the pit, and mash
the flesh with a fork. Stir in the
scallion, lemon juice, chili powder,
and chopped tomato. Set aside.

**2** Preheat the broiler.

**3** ▼ Handling the beef as little as
possible, divide it into 6 equal
portions. Shape each portion into a
¾-inch-thick patty and season.

**4** Arrange the patties on the rack in
the broiler pan. Broil about 3 inches
from the heat, 5 minutes on each side
for medium-rare, 8 minutes on each
side for well-done.

**5** ▲ Top each hamburger with a slice
of cheese and broil until melted, about
30 seconds.

**6** Set a hamburger in each toasted
bun. Top with a slice of tomato and a
spoonful of guacamole and serve.

# Chili con Carne

**SERVES 8**

3 tablespoons corn oil

1 large onion, chopped

2 pounds ground chuck

4 garlic cloves, minced

1 tablespoon light brown sugar

2-3 tablespoons chili powder

1 teaspoon ground cumin

1 teaspoon salt

1 teaspoon pepper

½ cup tomato paste

1 cup beer

2 cups tomato sauce

2 cups cooked or canned red kidney
   beans, rinsed and drained

FOR SERVING

1 pound spaghetti, broken in half

1 cup sour cream

2 cups shredded Monterey jack or
   cheddar cheese

**1** Heat the oil in a deep saucepan and
cook the onion until softened, about 5
minutes. Add the beef and cook until
browned, breaking up the meat with
the side of a spoon.

**2** ▼ Stir in the garlic, brown sugar,
chili powder, cumin, salt, and pepper.
Add the tomato paste, beer, and
tomato sauce and stir to mix. Bring to
a boil. Reduce the heat, cover, and
simmer 50 minutes.

**3** ▲ Stir in the kidney beans and
simmer 5 minutes longer, uncovered.

**4** Meanwhile, cook the spaghetti in a
large pot of boiling salted water until
just tender (check package directions
for cooking time). Drain.

**5** To serve, put the spaghetti into a
warmed bowl. Ladle the chili over the
spaghetti and top with some of the
sour cream and shredded cheese.
Serve the remaining sour cream and
cheese separately.

*Guacamole Cheeseburgers (top), Chili con Carne*

# Old-Fashioned Beef Stew

**SERVES 6**

3 tablespoons corn oil

1 large onion, sliced

2 carrots, chopped

1 celery stalk, chopped

2 tablespoons flour

3 tablespoons paprika

2 pounds beef chuck steak, cubed

2 tablespoons tomato paste

1 cup red wine

2 cups beef stock

1 sprig of fresh thyme or 1 teaspoon dried thyme

1 bay leaf

salt and pepper

3 medium potatoes, cut into 1½-inch pieces

1 cup button mushrooms, quartered

1  Preheat the oven to 375°F.

2 ▼  Heat half the oil in a large flameproof casserole. Add the onion, carrots, and celery and cook until softened, about 5 minutes. Remove the vegetables with a slotted spoon and set aside.

3 ▲  Combine the flour and paprika in a plastic bag. Add the beef cubes and shake to coat them with the seasoned flour.

4  Heat the remaining oil in the casserole. Add the beef cubes and brown well on all sides, about 10 minutes.

5  Return the vegetables to the casserole. Stir in the tomato paste, red wine, stock, thyme, bay leaf, and a little salt and pepper. Bring to a boil.

6 ▲  Stir in the potatoes. Cover the casserole and transfer it to the oven. Cook 1 hour.

7  Stir in the mushrooms and continue cooking until the beef is very tender, about 30 minutes longer. Discard the bay leaf before serving.

# Steak, Bell Pepper, and Corn Stir-Fry

**SERVES 4**

2–3 teaspoons chili powder

1 teaspoon ground cumin

½ teaspoon dried oregano

salt and pepper

1 pound beef top round steak, cut into thin strips

2 tablespoons corn oil

5 scallions, cut on the diagonal into 1-inch lengths

1 small green bell pepper, cored and thinly sliced

1 small red bell pepper, cored and thinly sliced

1 small yellow bell pepper, cored and thinly sliced

¼ pound baby corn, halved lengthwise, or 1 cup corn kernels

4 garlic cloves, minced

2 tablespoons fresh lime juice

2 tablespoons chopped fresh coriander leaves (cilantro)

**1** ▼ In a medium bowl, combine the spices, oregano, and a little salt and pepper. Rub the mixture into the steak strips.

**2** Heat half the oil in a wok or large frying pan over high heat. Add the steak strips and stir-fry until well browned on all sides, 3–4 minutes. Remove the steak from the wok with a slotted spoon and keep hot.

**3** ▲ Heat the remaining oil in the wok and add the scallions, bell peppers, corn, and garlic. Stir-fry until the vegetables are crisp-tender, about 3 minutes.

**4** ▼ Return the steak to the wok and toss briefly to mix with the vegetables and heat it through. Stir in the lime juice and coriander and serve.

# Corned Beef Boiled Dinner

**SERVES 6**

2–2½ pounds corned beef brisket

1 teaspoon black peppercorns

2 bay leaves

1 small rutabaga, about 1 pound, cut into pieces

8 small white onions, peeled

8 small red potatoes

3 carrots, cut into sticks

1 small head of green cabbage, cut into 6 wedges

FOR THE SAUCE

⅓ cup red wine vinegar

5 tablespoons sugar

1 tablespoon mustard powder

4–5 tablespoons butter or margarine

salt and pepper

**1** Put the brisket in a large pot. Add the peppercorns and bay leaves and cover with water. Bring to a boil. Reduce the heat and simmer until the beef is almost tender, about 2 hours.

**2 ▼** Add the rutabaga, onions, potatoes, and carrots. Bring the liquid back to a boil, then reduce the heat and cover the pot. Simmer 10 minutes.

**3** Add the cabbage wedges. Cover and cook 15 minutes longer.

**4** With a slotted spoon, remove the meat and vegetables from the pot and keep them hot. Reserve 1½ cups of the cooking liquid.

**5 ▲** For the sauce, combine the reserved cooking liquid, vinegar, sugar, and mustard in a small saucepan. Bring to a boil, then reduce the heat and simmer until thickened, about 5 minutes. Remove the pan from the heat and swirl in the butter or margarine. Season to taste with salt and pepper.

**6** Slice the beef and arrange with the vegetables on a warmed platter. Serve with the sauce in a sauceboat.

# Steak Sandwiches with Onions

**SERVES 3**

1 pound minute or sandwich steaks

salt and pepper

2 tablespoons butter or margarine

2 tablespoons corn oil

1 large onion, thinly sliced into rings

1 long flat loaf of Italian or French bread, split in half lengthwise, and cut into 3 sections

Dijon-style mustard, for serving

**1** Sprinkle the steaks generously with salt and pepper.

**2 ▲** Heat the butter or margarine and half of the oil in a frying pan. Add the onion and cook until browned and crispy, about 8 minutes. Remove the onion with a slotted spoon and drain on paper towels. Add the remaining oil to the pan.

**3 ▼** Add the steaks to the frying pan and cook until well browned, about 3 minutes, turning once.

**4** Divide the steak and onions among the bottom halves of the bread sections, and put on the tops. Serve on warmed plates with mustard.

*Corned Beef Boiled Dinner (top), Steak Sandwiches with Onions*

# Pork with Mustard-Peppercorn Sauce

**SERVES 4**

2 pork tenderloins, about ¾ pound each

2 tablespoons butter or margarine

1 tablespoon olive oil

1 tablespoon red wine vinegar

1 tablespoon whole-grain mustard

3 tablespoons whipping cream

1 tablespoon green peppercorns in brine, drained

pinch salt

**1** Cut the pork tenderloins across into 1-inch-thick slices.

**2** ▼ Heat the butter or margarine and oil in a frying pan. Add the slices of pork and fry until browned and cooked through, 5–8 minutes on each side. Transfer the pork to a warmed serving plate and keep hot.

**3** ▼ Add the vinegar and mustard to the pan and cook 1 minute, stirring with a wooden spoon to loosen any particles attached to the bottom.

**4** Stir in the cream, peppercorns, and salt. Boil 1 minute. Pour the sauce over the pork and serve immediately.

# Pork Chop, Potato, and Apple Scallop

**SERVES 6**

2 cups apple juice

½ pound baking potatoes, peeled and cut into ½-inch slices

½ pound sweet potatoes, peeled and cut into ½-inch slices

1 pound apples, peeled, cored, and cut into ½-inch slices

salt and pepper

6 tablespoons flour

6 pork chops, cut 1-inch thick, trimmed of excess fat

4 tablespoons butter or margarine

3 tablespoons corn oil

6 fresh sage leaves

**1** Preheat the oven to 350°F. Grease a 13- × 9-inch baking dish.

**2** In a small saucepan, bring the apple juice to a boil.

**3** ▼ Arrange a row of baking-potato slices at a short end of the prepared dish. Arrange a row of sweet-potato slices next to the first row, slightly overlapping it, and then a row of apple slices. Repeat the alternating overlapping rows to fill the dish. Sprinkle with salt and pepper.

**4** Pour the apple juice over the potato and apple slices. Cover the dish with foil and bake 40 minutes.

**5** ▲ Meanwhile, season the flour with salt and pepper. Coat the chops with the seasoned flour, shaking off any excess. Melt the butter or margarine with the oil in a frying pan. Fry the chops until well browned, about 5 minutes on each side.

**6** Uncover the baking dish. Arrange the chops on top of the potatoes and apples. Put a sage leaf on each chop.

**7** Return to the oven, uncovered, and cook until the potatoes and pork chops are tender and most of the liquid is absorbed, about 1 hour.

*Pork with Mustard-Peppercorn Sauce (top), Pork Chop, Potato, and Apple Scallop*

# Pork Chops with Sauerkraut

**SERVES 6**

6 bacon slices, coarsely chopped

3 tablespoons flour

salt and pepper

6 boned top-loin pork chops or sirloin cutlets

2 teaspoons light brown sugar

1 garlic clove, minced

1½ pounds sauerkraut, rinsed

1 teaspoon juniper berries

1 teaspoon black peppercorns

1 cup beer

1 cup chicken stock

**1** Preheat the oven to 350°F.

**2 ▼** In a frying pan, fry the bacon until just beginning to brown. With a slotted spoon, transfer the bacon to a casserole dish.

**3 ▲** Season the flour with salt and pepper. Coat the pork chops with the seasoned flour, shaking off any excess. Brown the chops in the bacon fat, about 5 minutes on each side. Remove and drain on paper towels.

**4 ▲** Add the brown sugar and garlic to the fat in the frying pan and cook, stirring, for 3 minutes. Add the sauerkraut, juniper berries, and peppercorns.

**5 ▲** Transfer the sauerkraut mixture to the casserole and mix with the bacon. Lay the pork chops on top. Pour the beer and chicken stock over the chops.

**6** Place the casserole in the oven and cook until the chops are very tender, 45–55 minutes.

# Barbecue Spareribs

**SERVES 4**

3 pounds meaty pork spareribs, in 2 pieces

½ cup corn oil

½ teaspoon paprika

FOR THE SAUCE

½ cup light brown sugar, firmly packed

2 teaspoons mustard powder

1 teaspoon salt

⅛ teaspoon pepper

½ teaspoon ground ginger

½ cup tomato sauce

½ cup fresh orange juice

1 small onion, finely chopped

1 garlic clove, minced

2 tablespoons chopped fresh parsley

1 tablespoon Worcestershire sauce

**1 ▲** Preheat the oven to 375°F. Arrange the ribs in one layer in a roasting pan.

**2 ▲** In a small bowl, combine the oil and paprika. Brush the mixture on the spareribs. Bake until the ribs are slightly crisp, 55–60 minutes.

**3 ▼** Combine the sauce ingredients in a saucepan and bring to a boil. Simmer 5 minutes, stirring occasionally.

**4 ▲** Pour off the fat from the roasting pan. Brush the ribs with half of the sauce and bake 20 minutes. Turn the ribs over and brush with the remaining sauce. Bake 20 minutes longer. Cut into sections for serving.

# Pork Tostadas

**SERVES 4**

1 garlic clove, minced

2 tablespoons corn oil

⅓ cup fresh lime juice

3 tablespoons Worcestershire sauce

⅛ teaspoon pepper

1¼ pounds pork cutlets, cut lengthwise into ⅜-inch-wide strips

1 large ripe avocado

½ cup loosely packed fresh coriander (cilantro) leaves, finely chopped

8 corn tortillas

1 onion, sliced

1 green bell pepper, seeded and sliced

black olives, for garnishing

**FOR THE SALSA**

1 cup cooked fresh or thawed frozen corn kernels

1 small red bell pepper, seeded and finely chopped

1 small red onion, thinly sliced

1 teaspoon honey

juice of 1 lime

**1 ▼** In a medium bowl, combine the garlic, 1 tablespoon of the oil, the lime juice, Worcestershire sauce, and pepper. Add the pork strips and toss to coat. Let marinate 10–20 minutes, stirring the strips at least once.

**2 ▲** Meanwhile, combine all the ingredients for the salsa in a bowl and mix well. Set aside.

**3 ▲** Cut the avocado in half and remove the pit. Scrape the flesh into a bowl and mash it with a fork. Stir in the chopped coriander.

**4 ▲** Preheat the oven to 350°F. Wrap the corn tortillas in foil and heat them in the oven for 10 minutes.

**5 ▲** Meanwhile, heat the remaining oil in a frying pan. Add the onion and green bell pepper slices and cook until softened, about 5 minutes.

**6 ▲** Add the pork strips to the frying pan and fry briskly, turning occasionally, until cooked and browned, about 5 minutes.

**7 ▲** To serve, place a spoonful of the avocado on each of the heated tortillas. Top with some of the pork mixture and a spoonful of the salsa. Garnish with an olive, and serve with more salsa if you like.

# Baked Sausages and Beans with Crispy Topping

**SERVES 6**

2 cups dry navy beans or Great Northern beans, soaked overnight and drained

1 onion, stuck with 4 cloves

3 tablespoons butter or margarine

1 pound pork link sausages

1 pound kielbasa sausage, cut into ½-inch slices

¼ pound bacon, chopped

1 large onion, finely chopped

2 garlic cloves, minced

1 16-ounce can crushed tomatoes

½ cup tomato paste

¼ cup maple syrup

2 tablespoons dark brown sugar

½ teaspoon mustard powder

¼ teaspoon salt

pepper

½ cup fresh bread crumbs

**1 ▲** Put the beans in a saucepan and cover with fresh cold water. Add the clove-studded onion. Bring to a boil and boil until the beans are just tender, about 1 hour. Drain the beans. Discard the onion.

**2** Preheat the oven to 350°F.

**3 ▲** Melt half of the butter or margarine in a large flameproof casserole. Add the sausages, bacon, onion, and garlic and fry until the bacon and sausages are well browned.

**4 ▲** Stir in the beans, tomatoes, tomato paste, maple syrup, brown sugar, mustard, salt, and pepper to taste. Bring to a boil.

**5 ▲** Sprinkle the bread crumbs over the surface and dot with the remaining butter or margarine.

**6** Transfer the casserole to the oven and bake until most of liquid has been absorbed by the beans and the top is crisp, about 1 hour.

# Jambalaya

**SERVES 6**

| |
|---|
| 2 tablespoons corn oil |
| 4 skinless boneless chicken breast halves, cut into chunks |
| 1 pound spicy cooked sausage, sliced |
| 6 ounces smoked ham, cubed |
| 1 large onion, chopped |
| 2 celery stalks, chopped |
| 2 green bell peppers, seeded and chopped |
| 3 garlic cloves, minced |
| 1 cup canned crushed tomatoes |
| 2 cups chicken stock |
| 1 teaspoon cayenne |
| 1 sprig of fresh thyme or ¼ teaspoon dried thyme |
| 2 sprigs of flat-leaf (Italian) parsley |
| 1 bay leaf |
| 1½ cups rice |
| salt and pepper |
| 4 scallions, finely chopped |

**1** ▼ Heat the oil in a large frying pan. Add the chicken chunks and sausage slices and cook until well browned, about 5 minutes. Stir in the ham cubes and cook 5 minutes longer.

**2** Add the onion, celery, bell peppers, garlic, tomatoes, stock, cayenne, thyme, parsley, and bay leaf to the frying pan. Bring to a boil, stirring well.

**3** ▲ Stir in the rice, and add salt and and pepper to taste. When the liquid returns to a boil, reduce the heat and cover the pan tightly. Simmer 10 minutes.

**4** Remove the pan from the heat and, without removing the lid, set aside for 20 minutes, to let the rice finish cooking.

**5** ▲ Discard the bay leaf. Scatter the chopped scallions on top of the jambalaya just before serving.

# Ham and Asparagus with Cheese Sauce

**SERVES 4**

24 asparagus spears

3 tablespoons butter or margarine

3 tablespoons flour

1½ cups milk

1 cup shredded Swiss cheese

⅛ teaspoon grated nutmeg

salt and pepper

12 thin slices of cooked ham or prosciutto

**1** Trim tough stalk ends from the asparagus. Bring a wide shallow pan of salted water to a boil. Add the asparagus and simmer until barely tender, 5–7 minutes. Drain the asparagus in a colander, rinse with cold water, and spread out on paper towels to dry.

**2** Preheat the broiler. Grease a 13- × 9-inch baking dish.

**3** Melt the butter or margarine in a saucepan. Add the flour and cook 2 minutes, stirring. Stir in the milk. Bring to a boil, stirring constantly, and simmer until thickened, about 5 minutes.

**4** ▲ Add ¾ cup of the cheese to the sauce. Season to taste with nutmeg, salt, and pepper. Keep warm.

**5** ▲ Wrap a pair of asparagus spears in each slice of ham. Arrange in the prepared baking dish, in one layer.

**6** Pour the sauce over the ham and asparagus rolls and sprinkle the remaining cheese on top. Broil about 3 inches from the heat until bubbling and golden brown, about 5 minutes. Serve hot.

---

# Ham Steaks with Raisin Sauce

**SERVES 4**

⅓ cup raisins

1 cup warm water

½ teaspoon instant coffee

1 teaspoon cornstarch

3 tablespoons butter or margarine

4 ham steaks, about ¼ pound each, trimmed of excess fat

2 teaspoons dark brown sugar

2 teaspoons cider vinegar

2 teaspoons soy sauce

**1** ▼ In a small bowl, soak the raisins in half of the water to plump them, about 10 minutes.

**2** Stir the coffee and cornstarch into the remaining water until smooth.

**3** Melt the butter or margarine in a large frying pan. Add the ham steaks and cook over medium-low heat until lightly browned, about 5 minutes on each side.

**4** ▲ Transfer the cooked steaks to a heated serving dish.

**5** Drain the raisins and add them to the frying pan. Stir the coffee mixture to recombine it, then add to the pan with the sugar, vinegar, and soy sauce. Bring to a boil and simmer until slightly thickened, about 3 minutes, stirring constantly.

**6** Spoon the raisin sauce over the ham steaks and serve.

~ **VARIATION** ~

For a richer sauce, substitute an equal quantity of chopped prunes for the raisins.

*Ham and Asparagus with Cheese Sauce (top), Ham Steaks with Raisin Sauce*

# Pesto Lamb Chops

**SERVES 4**

small bunch of fresh basil leaves

¼ cup pine nuts

2 garlic cloves, peeled

¼ cup freshly grated Parmesan cheese

½ cup extra-virgin olive oil

salt and pepper

4 lamb sirloin or blade chops, about ½ pound each

fresh basil sprigs, for garnishing

**1** In a food processor or blender, combine the basil, pine nuts, garlic, and Parmesan cheese. Process until the ingredients are finely chopped. Gradually pour in the olive oil in a thin stream. Season to taste with salt and pepper. The sauce should be thin and creamy. Alternatively, use a mortar and pestle to make the sauce.

**2 ▼** Put the lamb chops in a shallow dish that will hold them comfortably side by side. Pour the pesto sauce over the chops. Turn to coat on both sides. Let marinate 1 hour.

**3** Preheat the broiler. Brush the rack in the broiler pan with olive oil.

**4 ▲** Transfer the chops to the broiler rack. Broil about 3 inches from the heat until well browned and cooked to taste, about 15 minutes, turning once. Serve garnished with fresh basil sprigs.

# Lamb and Bean Stew

**SERVES 6**

1½ cups dried red kidney beans, soaked overnight and drained

2 tablespoons vegetable oil

2 pounds lean boned lamb, cut into 1½-inch cubes

1 large onion, chopped

1 bay leaf

3 cups chicken stock

1 garlic clove, minced

salt and pepper

**1** Put the beans in a large pot. Cover with fresh water, bring to a boil, and boil 10 minutes. Reduce the heat and simmer 30 minutes, then drain.

**2** Meanwhile, heat the oil in another large pot. Add the lamb cubes and fry until browned all over. Remove the lamb with a slotted spoon and reserve until needed.

**3 ▼** Add the onion to the hot oil and cook until softened, about 5 minutes.

**4 ▲** Return the lamb cubes to the pot and add the drained beans, bay leaf, stock, garlic, and salt and pepper to taste. Bring to a boil. Reduce the heat, cover, and simmer 1¼ hours, or until the lamb and beans are tender.

**5** Discard the bay leaf, and adjust the seasoning before serving.

*Pesto Lamb Chops (top), Lamb and Bean Stew*

# Sesame Lamb Chops

**SERVES 4**

8 lamb rib chops

salt and pepper

1 egg

1 teaspoon Dijon-style mustard

3 tablespoons fine dry bread crumbs

3 tablespoons sesame seeds

2 tablespoons flour

2 tablespoons butter or margarine

1 tablespoon oil

**1 ▼** If necessary, trim any excess fat from the chops. With a small knife, scrape all the meat and fat off the top 2 inches of the bone in each chop. Sprinkle the chops generously with salt and pepper.

**2 ▲** In a bowl, beat the egg and mustard together. Pour into a shallow dish. In another dish, mix the bread crumbs and sesame seeds. Place the flour in a third dish.

**3 ▲** Dredge each chop in flour, shaking off any excess. Dip in the egg and mustard mixture and then coat with the bread crumb mixture, pressing it on the meat to get an even coating. Refrigerate 15 minutes.

**4 ▲** Heat the butter or margarine and oil in a frying pan. Add the chops and fry over medium heat until crisp and golden and cooked to taste, 4–5 minutes on each side, turning gently with tongs.

# Roast Rack of Lamb

**Serves 4**

2 racks of lamb, each with 8 chops, ends of bones scraped clean

¼ cup Dijon-style mustard

1½ tablespoons fresh rosemary or 1 tablespoon dried rosemary

salt and pepper

½ cup fine dry bread crumbs

¼ cup chopped fresh parsley

4 garlic cloves, minced

¼ cup olive oil

½ cup butter or margarine

1 cup chicken stock

**1** Preheat the oven to 425°F.

**2** ▲ Brush the meaty side of the racks with the mustard. Sprinkle with the rosemary, salt, and pepper.

**3** ▲ In a bowl, mix the bread crumbs with the parsley, garlic, and half of the olive oil. Press this mixture evenly over the mustard on the racks of lamb. Wrap the scraped bone ends with foil. Put the racks in a roasting pan.

**4** In a small saucepan, melt half the butter or margarine. Stir in the remaining olive oil. Drizzle this mixture over the crumb coating.

**5** Roast the racks of lamb, allowing 40 minutes for medium-rare meat and 50 minutes for medium.

**6** Transfer the racks to a warmed serving platter, arranging them so the scraped ends of the bones are interlocked. Cover loosely with foil and set aside.

**7** Pour the stock into the roasting pan and bring to a boil, scraping the bottom of the pan with a wooden spoon to mix in all the cooking juices. Remove from the heat and swirl in the remaining butter or margarine. Pour the gravy into a warmed sauceboat.

**8** To serve, carve each rack by cutting down between the chop bones, or cut down after every 2 bones for double chops.

# Glazed Lamb Kabobs

**SERVES 4**

1 pound boned leg of lamb, cut into 1-inch cubes

3 medium zucchini, cut into ½-inch slices

¼ cup mint jelly

2 tablespoons fresh lemon juice

2 tablespoons olive oil

1 tablespoon chopped fresh mint

~ VARIATION ~

Substitute an equal quantity of orange marmalade for the mint jelly. Instead of fresh mint, use 2 teaspoons of grated orange rind.

1  Preheat the broiler.

2  Thread the cubes of lamb and slices of zucchini alternately onto metal or wooden skewers.

3 ▲ Combine the mint jelly, lemon juice, olive oil, and chopped mint in a small saucepan. Stir over low heat until the jelly melts.

4 ▼ Brush the lamb and zucchini with the mint glaze. Lay them on the rack in the broiler pan.

5  Cook under the broiler, about 3 inches from the heat, until browned and cooked to taste, 10–12 minutes, turning the skewers frequently. Serve on a bed of rice, if wished.

---

# Lamb Burgers with Cucumber-Mint Relish

**SERVES 4**

1½ pounds ground lamb

1 medium onion, finely chopped

1 tablespoon paprika

2 tablespoons chopped fresh parsley

2 tablespoons chopped fresh mint or 1 tablespoon dried mint

salt and pepper

4 hamburger buns with sesame seeds, split open

FOR THE RELISH

2 medium hothouse cucumbers, thinly sliced

1 small red onion, thinly sliced

3 tablespoons fresh lime juice

2 teaspoons vegetable oil

½ cup chopped fresh mint or 2 tablespoons dried mint

2 scallions, finely chopped

1  To make the relish, combine the cucumbers, red onion, lime juice, oil, mint, and scallions in a non-metallic bowl. Cover the mixture and refrigerate at least 2 hours.

2 ▲ In a bowl, combine the lamb, onion, paprika, parsley, mint, and a little salt and pepper. Mix thoroughly.

3  Preheat the broiler.

4 ▲ Divide the lamb mixture into 4 equal portions and shape each into a 1-inch-thick patty.

5  Broil the burgers, about 3 inches from the heat, allowing 5 minutes on each side for medium and 8 minutes on each side for well-done. At the same time, toast the cut surfaces of the buns briefly under the broiler.

6  Serve the lamb burgers in the buns, with the cucumber-mint relish.

*Glazed Lamb Kabobs (top), Lamb Burgers with Cucumber-Mint Relish*

# Chicken Breasts with Prunes and Almonds

**SERVES 4**

2 tablespoons butter or margarine

1 tablespoon corn oil

2½ pounds chicken breast halves

3 cups chicken stock

⅔ cup raisins

1 tablespoon fresh thyme leaves or 1 teaspoon dried thyme

3 fresh sage leaves, chopped

¼ cup chopped fresh parsley

1 tablespoon chopped fresh marjoram or 1 teaspoon dried marjoram

1 cup fresh bread crumbs

½ cup ground almonds

12 prunes, pitted

4–6 whole cloves

½ teaspoon ground mace

pinch of saffron threads, crumbled

salt and pepper

⅓ cup sliced almonds, toasted

**1 ▼** Melt the butter or margarine with the oil in a frying pan. Add the chicken and brown 10 minutes, turning once. Transfer the chicken pieces to a large pot.

~ COOK'S TIP ~

For ground almonds, chop whole or slivered almonds in a food processor until powdery.

**2 ▲** Pour the stock into the pot and bring to a boil. Add all the remaining ingredients, except the toasted almonds, and stir well to mix. Simmer 45 minutes.

**3 ▲** With tongs, remove the chicken from the pot and let cool. Bring the cooking liquid back to a boil and boil until well reduced, about 10 minutes, stirring frequently.

**4 ▲** Remove the bones from the chicken and return the meat to the sauce. Heat through. Serve sprinkled with the toasted almonds.

# Southern Fried Chicken

**SERVES 4**

½ cup buttermilk

1 3-pound chicken, cut into pieces

corn oil for frying

½ cup flour

1 tablespoon paprika

¼ teaspoon pepper

1 tablespoon water

**1 ▼** Pour the buttermilk into a large bowl and add the chicken pieces. Stir to coat, then set aside for 5 minutes.

**2** Heat a ¼-inch layer of oil in a large frying pan over medium-high heat. Do not let oil overheat.

**3 ▲** In a bowl or plastic bag, combine the flour, paprika, and pepper. One by one, lift the chicken pieces out of the buttermilk and dip into the flour to coat all over, shaking off any excess.

**4 ▼** Add the chicken pieces to the hot oil and fry until lightly browned, about 10 minutes, turning over halfway through cooking time.

**5 ▲** Reduce the heat to low and add the water to the frying pan. Cover and cook 30 minutes, turning the pieces over at 10-minute intervals. Uncover the pan and continue cooking until the chicken is very tender and the coating is crisp, about 15 minutes, turning every 5 minutes. Serve hot.

# Honey Roast Chicken

SERVES 4

| |
|---|
| 1 3½-pound chicken |
| 2 tablespoons clear honey |
| 1 tablespoon brandy |
| 1½ tablespoons flour |
| ⅔ cup chicken stock |
| FOR THE STUFFING |
| 2 shallots, chopped |
| 4 bacon slices, chopped |
| ½ cup button mushrooms, quartered |
| 1 tablespoon butter or margarine |
| 2 thick slices of white bread, diced |
| 1 tablespoon chopped fresh parsley |
| salt and pepper |

**1 ▼** For the stuffing, gently fry the shallots, bacon, and mushrooms in a frying pan for 5 minutes. With a slotted spoon, transfer them to a bowl.

**2** Pour off all but 2 tablespoons of bacon fat from the pan. Add the butter or margarine to the pan and fry the bread until golden brown. Add the bread to the bacon mixture. Stir in the parsley and salt and pepper to taste. Let cool.

**3** Preheat the oven to 350°F.

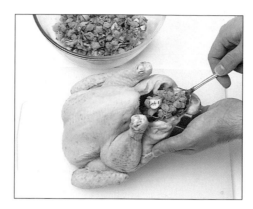

**4 ▲** Pack the stuffing into the body cavity of the chicken. Truss it with string, or secure with poultry pins, to keep it in a neat shape.

**5 ▲** Transfer the chicken to a roasting pan which just holds it comfortably.

**6 ▲** Mix the honey with the brandy. Brush half of the mixture over the chicken. Roast until the chicken is thoroughly cooked, about 1 hour 20 minutes. Baste the chicken frequently with the remaining honey mixture during roasting.

**7 ▲** Transfer the chicken to a warmed serving platter. Cover with foil and set aside.

**8 ▲** Strain the cooking juices into a degreasing pitcher. Set aside to let the fat rise to the surface.

**9 ▲** Stir the flour into the sediments in the roasting pan. Add the lean part of the juices and the stock. Boil rapidly until the gravy has thickened, stirring constantly.

**10** Pour the gravy into a warmed sauceboat and serve with the chicken.

# Chicken Thighs Wrapped in Bacon

**SERVES 4**

16 bacon slices

8 chicken thighs, skin removed

FOR THE MARINADE

finely grated rind and juice of 1 orange

finely grated rind and juice of 1 lime

5 garlic cloves, minced

1 tablespoon chili powder

1 tablespoon paprika

1 teaspoon ground cumin

½ teaspoon dried oregano

1 tablespoon olive oil

**1** For the marinade, combine the citrus rind and juice, garlic, chili powder, paprika, cumin, oregano, and olive oil in a bowl.

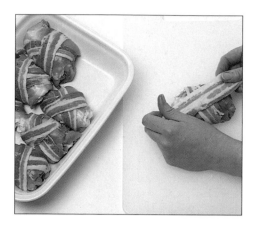

**2 ▲** Wrap 2 slices of bacon around each chicken thigh in a cross shape. Secure with wooden toothpicks. Arrange the wrapped chicken thighs in a baking dish.

**3** Pour the marinade over the chicken, cover, and let marinate 1 hour at room temperature or several hours in the refrigerator.

**4** Preheat the oven to 375°F.

**5 ▼** Put the baking dish in the oven and bake until the chicken is cooked through and the bacon is crisp, about 40 minutes for small thighs and 1 hour for large thighs. Skim excess fat from the sauce before serving. Rice is a good accompaniment because there is plenty of sauce.

# Deviled Chicken Drumsticks

**SERVES 4**

2 tablespoons corn oil

8 chicken drumsticks, about 3 pounds

1 medium onion, chopped

½ cup water

¼ cup Dijon-style mustard

1 tablespoon prepared horseradish

1 tablespoon Worcestershire sauce

1 teaspoon light brown sugar

¼ teaspoon salt

parsley sprigs, for garnishing

**1** Heat the oil in a frying pan. Add the chicken drumsticks and brown them on all sides. With a spatula or tongs, remove the drumsticks from the pan and drain on paper towels.

**2 ▲** Add the onion to the hot oil and cook until softened, about 5 minutes. Return the chicken to the pan. Stir in the water, mustard, horseradish, Worcestershire sauce, brown sugar, and salt. Bring to a boil.

**3** Reduce the heat to low. Cover the pan and simmer until the chicken is very tender, about 45 minutes, stirring occasionally.

**4 ▼** Transfer the drumsticks to a warmed serving dish. Skim any fat off the cooking juices. Pour the juices over the chicken. Garnish with parsley and serve.

*Chicken Thighs Wrapped in Bacon (top), Deviled Chicken Drumsticks*

# Cornish Game Hens with Cranberry Sauce

**SERVES 4**

4 Cornish game hens, with giblets, each
about 1 pound

3 tablespoons butter or margarine

salt and pepper

1 onion, quartered

¼ cup port wine

⅔ cup chicken stock

2 tablespoons honey

1½ cups fresh cranberries

---

~ **VARIATION** ~

For extra zest, add 2 tablespoons
of finely grated orange rind to
the sauce with the cranberries.

---

**1** Preheat the oven to 450°F.

**2** ▼ Smear the hens on all sides with
2 tablespoons of the butter or
margarine. Arrange them, on their
sides, in a roasting pan in which they
will fit comfortably. Sprinkle them
with salt and pepper. Add the onion
quarters to the pan. Chop the gizzards
and livers and arrange them around
the hens.

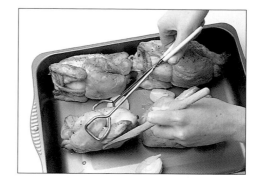

**3** ▲ Roast 20 minutes, basting often
with the melted fat in the pan. Turn
the hens onto their other sides and
roast 20 minutes longer, basting often.
Turn the hens breast up and continue
roasting until they are cooked
through, about 15 minutes. Transfer
the hens to a warmed serving dish.
Cover with foil and set aside.

**4** Skim any fat off the juices in the
roasting pan. Put the pan on top of
the stove and bring the juices to a
boil. Add the port wine and bring
back to a boil, stirring well to dislodge
any particles attached to the bottom
of the pan.

**5** ▲ Strain the sauce into a small
saucepan. Add the stock, bring to a
boil, and boil until reduced by half.
Stir in the honey and cranberries.
Simmer until the cranberries pop,
about 3 minutes.

**6** Remove the pan from the heat and
swirl in the remaining butter or
margarine. Season to taste with salt
and pepper. Pour the sauce into a
sauceboat and serve with the hens.

# Barbecue Chicken

**SERVES 4**

3 tablespoons corn oil

1 large onion, chopped

¾ cup catsup

¾ cup water

2½ tablespoons fresh lemon juice

1½ tablespoons prepared horseradish

1 tablespoon light brown sugar

1 tablespoon spicy brown mustard

3 pounds chicken pieces

**1** Preheat the oven to 350°F.

**2** ▲ Heat 1 tablespoon of the oil in a saucepan. Add the onion and cook until softened, about 5 minutes. Stir in the catsup, water, lemon juice, horseradish, brown sugar, and mustard and bring to a boil. Reduce the heat and simmer the sauce 10 minutes, stirring occasionally.

**3** ▲ Heat the remaining oil in a heavy frying pan. Add the chicken pieces and brown on all sides. Drain the chicken pieces on paper towels.

**4** ▼ Transfer the chicken pieces to a 11- × 1-inch baking dish and pour the sauce over the top.

**5** ▲ Bake until the chicken is cooked and tender, about 1¼ hours, basting occasionally. Alternatively, grill over medium coals for 40–50 minutes, turning once and brushing frequently with the sauce.

# Chicken Potpie

| |
| --- |
| 4 tablespoons butter or margarine |
| 1 medium onion, chopped |
| 3 carrots, cut into ½-inch dice |
| 1 parsnip, cut into ½-inch dice |
| 3 tablespoons flour |
| 1½ cups chicken stock |
| ⅓ cup medium sherry wine |
| ⅓ cup dry white wine |
| ¾ cup whipping cream |
| ⅔ cup frozen peas, thawed and well drained |
| 3 cups cooked chicken meat, in chunks |
| 1 teaspoon dried thyme |
| 1 tablespoon minced fresh parsley |
| salt and pepper |
| FOR THE CRUST |
| 1⅓ cups flour |
| ½ teaspoon salt |
| ½ cup shortening |
| 2–3 tablespoons ice water |
| 1 egg |
| 2 tablespoons milk |

**1 ▲** For the crust, sift the flour and salt into a mixing bowl. Using a pastry blender, cut in the shortening until the mixture resembles coarse crumbs. Sprinkle in the water, 1 tablespoon at a time, tossing lightly with a fork until the dough will form a ball. Remove the dough, dust with flour, wrap, and refrigerate until required.

**2** Preheat the oven to 400°F.

**3 ▲** Heat half of the butter or margarine in a medium saucepan. Add the onion, carrots, and parsnip and cook until softened, about 10 minutes. Remove the vegetables from the pan with a slotted spoon.

**4 ▲** Melt the remaining butter or margarine in the saucepan. Add the flour and cook 5 minutes, stirring constantly. Stir in the stock, sherry, and white wine. Bring the sauce to a boil, and continue boiling for 1 minute, stirring constantly.

**5 ▲** Add the cream, peas, chicken, thyme, and parsley to the sauce. Season to taste with salt and pepper. Simmer 1 minute, stirring.

**6 ▼** Transfer the chicken mixture to a 2-quart shallow baking dish.

**7** On a lightly floured surface, roll out the dough to ½-inch thickness. Lay the dough over the baking dish and trim off the excess. Dampen the rim of the dish. With a fork, press the crust to the rim to seal.

**8** Cut decorative shapes from the dough trimmings.

**9 ▲** Lightly whisk the egg with the milk. Brush the pie crust all over with the egg wash. Arrange the dough shapes in an attractive design on top. Brush again with the egg wash. Make 1 or 2 holes in the crust so steam can escape during baking.

**10** Bake the pie until the pastry is golden brown, about 35 minutes. Serve hot.

# Chicken with Sweet Potatoes

**SERVES 6**

grated rind and juice of 1 large navel
    orange

⅓ cup soy sauce

1-inch piece of fresh gingerroot, peeled
    and finely grated

¼ teaspoon pepper

2½ pounds chicken pieces

½ cup flour

3 tablespoons corn oil

2 tablespoons butter or margarine

2 pounds sweet potatoes, peeled and cut
    into 1-inch pieces

3 tablespoons light brown sugar

**1** ▲ In a plastic bag, combine the orange rind and juice, soy sauce, gingerroot, and pepper. Add the chicken pieces. Put the bag in a mixing bowl (this will keep the chicken immersed in the marinade), and seal. Let marinate in the refrigerator overnight.

**2** Preheat the oven to 425°F.

**3** ▼ Drain the chicken, reserving the marinade. Coat the pieces with flour, shaking off any excess.

**4** Heat 2 tablespoons of the oil in a frying pan. Add the chicken pieces and brown on all sides. Drain.

**5** Put the remaining oil and the butter or margarine in a 12- × 9-inch baking dish. Heat in the oven a few minutes.

**6** ▲ Put the potato pieces in the bottom of the dish, tossing well to coat with the butter and oil. Arrange the chicken pieces in a single layer on top of the potatoes. Cover with foil and bake 40 minutes.

**7** Mix the reserved marinade with the brown sugar. Remove the foil from the baking dish and pour the marinade mixture over the chicken and potatoes. Bake uncovered until the chicken and potatoes are cooked through and tender, about 20 minutes.

# Chicken Tacos

**SERVES 4**

| |
|---|
| 1 3-pound chicken |
| 1 teaspoon salt |
| 12 taco shells |
| 1½ cups shredded lettuce |
| 1 cup chopped tomatoes |
| 1 cup sour cream |
| 1 cup shredded sharp cheddar cheese |

**FOR THE TACO SAUCE**

| |
|---|
| 1 cup tomato sauce |
| 1–2 garlic cloves, minced |
| ½ teaspoon cider vinegar |
| ½ teaspoon dried oregano |
| ½ teaspoon ground cumin |
| 1–2 tablespoons chili powder |

**1** Put the chicken in a large pot and add the salt and enough water to cover. Bring to a boil. Reduce the heat and simmer until the chicken is thoroughly cooked, about 45 minutes. Remove the chicken from the pot and let cool. Reserve ½ cup of the chicken stock for the sauce.

**2 ▲** Remove the chicken meat from the bones, discarding all skin. Chop the meat coarsely.

**3** For the sauce, combine all the ingredients with the stock in a saucepan and bring to a boil. Stir in the chicken meat. Simmer until the sauce thickens considerably, about 20 minutes, stirring occasionally.

**4** Preheat the oven to 350°F.

**5 ▲** Spread out the taco shells on 2 baking sheets. Heat in the oven for 7 minutes.

**6** Meanwhile, put the shredded lettuce, chopped tomatoes, sour cream, and shredded cheese in individual serving dishes.

**7 ▲** To serve, spoon a little of the chicken mixture into each taco shell. Garnish with the lettuce, tomatoes, sour cream, and cheese.

# Roast Turkey with Middle-Eastern Stuffing

**SERVES 12**

| |
|---|
| 1 12-pound turkey, with giblets |
| ¾ cup softened butter or margarine |
| salt and pepper |
| 1 lemon, quartered |
| 2 onions, quartered |
| 2 cups cold water |
| 6 eggplants, 3–4 inches long (optional) |
| 1 tablespoon cornstarch |
| parsley sprigs, for garnishing |
| FOR THE STUFFING |
| ¼ cup pine nuts |
| 1 cup couscous |
| 1¼ cups boiling water |
| 2 tablespoons butter or margarine |
| 6 scallions, chopped |
| 1 red bell pepper, seeded and chopped |
| ⅓ cup raisins |
| ½ teaspoon ground cumin |
| 3 tablespoons chopped fresh parsley |
| 1 tablespoon fresh lemon juice |

**1** Preheat the oven to 325°F. Put the pine nuts on a baking sheet and in the oven until golden brown, about 5–10 minutes, stirring occasionally.

**2** For the stuffing, put the couscous into a large bowl and pour the boiling water over it. Let stand 10 minutes.

**3** ▲ Add the pine nuts to the couscous with the rest of the stuffing ingredients. Mix with a fork to keep the grains of couscous separate.

**4** Rinse the turkey inside and out with cold water. Pat dry. Gently slide your hand under the breast skin and loosen it from the meat.

**5** ▲ Spread ½ cup of the softened butter or margarine under the skin all over the breast meat.

**6** Fill the neck end of the turkey with stuffing without packing it down. Reserve any remaining stuffing to serve apart. Sew the neck flap with a trussing needle and thread or secure with poultry pins.

**7** ▲ Sprinkle the body cavity with salt and pepper. Put the quartered lemon and one of the onions inside. Tie the legs together with string.

**8** Smear the remaining butter or margarine all over the turkey. Wrap it loosely in foil and set in a roasting pan. Roast, allowing 25 minutes per pound. Remove the foil for the last 30 minutes of roasting. To test for doneness, pierce the thigh with the tip of a sharp knife; the juices that run out should be clear.

**9** ▲ Meanwhile, put the giblets in a saucepan with the remaining onion and the water. Bring to a boil, simmer 1 hour, and strain.

**10** If using, halve the eggplants and steam until tender, about 10 minutes. Scoop out the inside, leaving a thick shell, and fill with the remaining stuffing. Alternatively, serve the remaining stuffing apart.

**11** When the turkey is done, transfer it to a warmed serving platter. Cover with foil and let rest 30 minutes.

**12** ▲ Skim the fat off the drippings in the roasting pan. Stir the cornstarch into a little of the giblet stock until smooth. Add the remaining giblet stock to the roasting pan, then stir in the cornstarch mixture. Bring to a boil, scraping the bottom of the pan well with a wooden spoon. Simmer 15 minutes. Strain the gravy, and adjust the seasoning.

**13** Garnish the turkey with the stuffed eggplants, if using, and parsley sprigs, and serve the gravy in a warmed sauceboat.

# Sliced Turkey Sandwich

SERVES 4

4 tablespoons butter or margarine

1 shallot, finely chopped

½ pound button mushrooms, quartered

1¼ pounds roasted turkey breast

4 thick slices of whole-wheat bread

2 cups thick turkey gravy

parsley sprigs, for garnishing

**1** Melt half the butter or margarine in a frying pan. Add the shallot and cook until softened, about 5 minutes.

~ **VARIATION** ~

If preferred, the sandwich bread may be toasted and buttered.

**2** Add the mushrooms and cook until the moisture they render has evaporated, about 5 minutes, stirring occasionally.

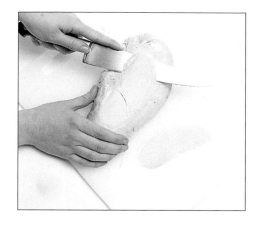

**3** ▲ Meanwhile, skin the turkey breast, and carve into 4 thick slices.

**4** In a saucepan, reheat the turkey gravy. Stir in the shallot and mushrooms.

**5** ▲ Spread the slices of bread with the remaining butter or margarine. Set a slice on each of 4 plates and top with the turkey slices. Pour the mushroom gravy over the turkey and serve hot, garnished with parsley.

# Leftover Turkey Casserole

SERVES 6

½ cup corn oil

4 eggs

2 cups milk

1 cup flour

salt and pepper

1½ pounds cooked turkey meat, cubed

½ cup thick plain yogurt

3 cups cornflakes, crushed

**1** Preheat the oven to 425°F.

**2** Pour the oil into a 13- × 9-inch baking dish. Heat in the oven about 10 minutes.

**3** Meanwhile, beat the eggs in a mixing bowl. Add the milk. Sift in the flour, and add a little salt and pepper. Mix until the batter is smooth. Set aside.

**4** ▲ Coat the turkey cubes in the yogurt, then roll in the crushed cornflakes to coat all over.

**5** ▲ Remove the baking dish from the oven and pour in the prepared batter. Arrange the turkey pieces on top. Return to the oven and bake until the batter is set and golden, 35–40 minutes. Serve hot.

*Sliced Turkey Sandwich (top), Leftover Turkey Casserole*

# Turkey Kiev

**SERVES 4**

4 turkey cutlets (boneless slices of breast), about 6 ounces each

salt and pepper

½ cup butter or margarine, chilled

1 teaspoon grated orange rind

2 tablespoons chopped fresh chives

flour, for dredging

3 eggs, beaten

1 cup fine dry bread crumbs

corn oil, for frying

orange wedges and parsley, for garnishing

**1** ▼ Place each cutlet between 2 sheets of wax paper. With the flat side of a meat pounder, pound until about ¼-inch thick, being careful not to split the meat. Remove the wax paper. Sprinkle the cutlets with salt and pepper.

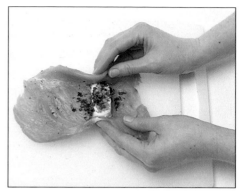

**2** ▲ Cut the butter or margarine into 4 finger-shaped pieces. Place a piece crosswise in the middle of a cutlet. Sprinkle with a little orange rind and chives.

**3** ▲ Fold in the 2 long sides of the cutlet, then roll up from a short end. Secure with wooden toothpicks. Repeat with the remaining cutlets.

**4** Dredge each roll lightly with flour, shaking off any excess. Dip in the beaten eggs, then roll in the bread crumbs to coat evenly on all sides. Refrigerate 1 hour to set the breaded coating.

**5** Pour enough oil into a frying pan to make a ½-inch layer and heat. Add the breaded turkey rolls to the hot oil and fry until crisp and golden on all sides, 15–20 minutes, turning gently with tongs.

**6** Remove the toothpicks before serving. Garnish with orange wedges and parsley.

# Turkey Scaloppine with Lemon and Sage

## SERVES 4

4 turkey cutlets (boneless slices of breast), about 6 ounces each

salt and pepper

1 tablespoon freshly grated lemon rind

1 tablespoon chopped fresh sage or 1 teaspoon dried sage

¼ cup fresh lemon juice

6 tablespoons vegetable oil

1 cup fine dry bread crumbs

fresh sage leaves, for garnishing

lemon slices, for garnishing

1 Place each cutlet between 2 sheets of wax paper. With the flat side of a meat pounder, pound until about ¼-inch thick, being careful not to split the meat. Remove the wax paper. Sprinkle the cutlets with salt and pepper.

2 ▲ In a small bowl, combine the lemon rind, sage, lemon juice, and 2 tablespoons of the oil. Stir well to mix.

~ VARIATION ~

For a delicious alternative, substitute fresh tarragon leaves for the sage.

3 ▼ Arrange the turkey cutlets, in one layer, in 1 or 2 shallow baking dishes. Divide the lemon mixture evenly between the dishes and rub well into the turkey. Let marinate 20 minutes.

4 ▲ Heat the remaining oil in a frying pan. Dredge the turkey scaloppine in the bread crumbs, shaking off the excess. Fry in the hot oil until golden brown, about 2 minutes on each side. Serve garnished with sage leaves and lemon slices.

# Turkey Chili

**SERVES 8**

2 tablespoons corn oil

1 medium onion, halved and thinly sliced

1 green bell pepper, seeded and diced

3 garlic cloves, minced

2 pounds ground turkey

2–3 tablespoons chili powder

1½ teaspoons ground cumin

1 teaspoon dried oregano

1 16-ounce can crushed tomatoes

2 tablespoons tomato paste

1 cup chicken stock

1 16-ounce can red kidney beans, drained and rinsed

¼ teaspoon salt

**1** Heat the oil in a large saucepan over medium heat. Add the onion, green bell pepper, and garlic and cook until softened, about 5 minutes, stirring frequently.

**2** ▼ Add the turkey and cook until it is lightly browned, about 5 minutes longer, stirring to break up the meat.

**3** ▼ Stir in the chili powder, cumin, and oregano. Add the tomatoes, tomato paste, chicken stock, kidney beans, and salt, and stir well.

**4** Bring to a boil, then reduce the heat and simmer 30 minutes, stirring occasionally. Serve the chili with boiled rice.

# Turkey Tetrazzini

**SERVES 4**

5 tablespoons butter or margarine

4 cups thinly sliced mushrooms

¼ cup flour

1¾ cups milk

2 cups chicken stock

¼ cup dry white wine

10 ounces spaghetti

3 cups chopped cooked turkey meat

1 cup frozen peas, thawed and drained

⅔ cup freshly grated Parmesan cheese

salt and pepper

⅓ cup fine fresh bread crumbs

**1** Preheat the oven to 375°F. Grease a shallow 3-quart baking dish.

**2** ▲ Melt 4 tablespoons of the butter or margarine in a medium saucepan. Add the mushrooms and cook 5 minutes, stirring frequently. Stir in the flour and cook 3 minutes, stirring constantly. Pour in the milk, stock, and white wine and bring to a boil, stirring. Reduce the heat and simmer 5 minutes.

**3** Meanwhile, cook the spaghetti in a large pot of boiling salted water until just tender (see package directions for suggested cooking time). Drain.

**4** ▼ Transfer the spaghetti to a mixing bowl. Pour in the mushroom sauce and mix well. Stir in the turkey, peas, ⅓ cup of the Parmesan, and salt and pepper to taste. Transfer the mixture to the baking dish.

**5** In a small bowl, combine the remaining Parmesan with the bread crumbs. Sprinkle evenly over the turkey mixture. Dot with the remaining butter or margarine, cut into pieces. Bake until bubbling and golden, 30–40 minutes. Serve hot, in the baking dish.

*Turkey Chili (top), Turkey Tetrazzini*

# PASTA, PIZZA & GRAINS

~

Versatile pasta and grains – rice, couscous, and bulgur wheat
– star in the recipes here, with a myriad of tasty sauces and
flavorings, for first courses or main dishes. And there are
pizzas with mouthwatering toppings.

# Spicy Cheese Lasagne

**SERVES 8**

½ pound lasagne noodles

4 tablespoons butter or margarine

1 large onion, finely chopped

3 garlic cloves, minced

1½ tablespoons chopped fresh green chili pepper

½ cup flour

4 cups milk

3 cups canned crushed tomatoes

1 large zucchini, sliced

½ teaspoon hot red pepper flakes

salt and pepper

3 cups shredded sharp cheddar cheese

**1** Preheat the oven to 375°F. Grease a 9- × 13-inch baking dish.

**2** Put the lasagne noodles, one at a time, in a bowl of hot water, and let soak for 10–15 minutes.

**3** ▲ Melt the butter or margarine in a large saucepan. Add the onion, garlic, and chili pepper and cook until softened, about 5 minutes.

**4** Stir in the flour and cook 3 minutes, stirring constantly. Pour in the milk and bring to a boil, stirring. Reduce the heat to low and simmer gently until thickened, about 5 minutes, stirring occasionally.

**5** Stir the tomatoes, zucchini, and hot pepper flakes into the sauce. Season with salt and pepper.

**6** Spoon a little of the sauce into the prepared baking dish and spread it out evenly over the bottom. Cover with a layer of noodles.

**7** ▲ Add one-third of the remaining sauce and one-third of the cheese. Repeat the layers until all the ingredients are used.

**8** Bake until the top is golden and bubbling, about 45 minutes. Serve hot, in the dish.

# Spaghetti with Sun-Dried Tomato Sauce

**SERVES 4**

¾ pound spaghetti

4 garlic cloves, minced

10–15 sun-dried tomatoes packed in oil, drained and chopped

1 cup pitted black olives

½ cup extra-virgin olive oil

3 beefsteak tomatoes, peeled, seeded, and chopped

3 tablespoons capers, drained

¼ cup chopped fresh basil, plus leaves for garnishing, or 1 teaspoon dried basil

salt and pepper

**1** Cook the spaghetti in a large pan of boiling salted water until just tender to the bite (check package directions for timing). Drain well.

**2** ▲ In a food processor or blender, combine the garlic, sun-dried tomatoes, and half the olives. Process until finely chopped.

**3** With the motor running, slowly add the olive oil. Continue processing until thickened.

**4** ▼ Transfer the mixture to a mixing bowl. Stir in the fresh tomatoes, capers, and basil. Season with salt and pepper to taste.

**5** Return the spaghetti to the saucepan and add the tomato sauce. Toss well. Serve immediately, garnished with the remaining olives and fresh basil leaves, if wished.

*Spicy Cheese Lasagne (top), Spaghetti with Sun-Dried Tomato Sauce*

# Pasta with Fresh Pesto Sauce

**SERVES 4**

1 cup chopped fresh basil, firmly packed

½ cup chopped fresh parsley

½ cup freshly grated Parmesan cheese

2 garlic cloves, peeled

4 tablespoons butter or margarine, at room temperature

¼ cup extra-virgin olive oil

salt

¾ pound mixed green and white fettucine or tagliatelle

½ cup pine nuts, toasted

fresh basil leaves, for garnishing

~ **COOK'S TIP** ~

For the best flavor, use a fruity olive oil in this recipe.

**1 ▲** In a food processor or blender, combine the basil, parsley, Parmesan, and garlic. Process until finely chopped.

**2** Add the butter or margarine and process to mix well.

**3 ▼** With the machine running, slowly add the olive oil. Season with salt to taste.

**4** Cook the pasta in a large pan of boiling salted water until just tender to the bite (check package directions for timing). Drain well.

**5** Toss the hot pasta with the pesto sauce. Sprinkle with the pine nuts, garnish with basil, and serve.

---

# Penne with Eggplant and Goat Cheese

**SERVES 6**

1¼ pounds eggplant, cut in ½-inch cubes (about 2 cups)

salt and pepper

3 tablespoons olive oil

1 tablespoon butter or margarine

1 garlic clove, chopped

2 cups canned crushed tomatoes

¾ pound penne (quill-shaped pasta)

¼ pound Montrachet or other firm goat cheese, cubed

3 tablespoons shredded fresh basil, or 1 teaspoon dried basil

**1** Put the eggplant cubes in a large colander and sprinkle them lightly with salt. Let drain at least 30 minutes.

**2** Rinse the eggplant under cold water and drain well. Dry on paper towels.

**3** Heat the oil and butter or margarine in a large saucepan. Add the eggplant cubes and fry until just golden on all sides, stirring frequently.

**4 ▲** Stir in the garlic and tomatoes. Simmer until thickened, about 15 minutes. Season with salt and pepper.

**5 ▲** Cook the penne in a large pan of boiling salted water until just tender to the bite (check package directions for timing). Drain well and transfer to a warmed serving bowl.

**6** Add the eggplant sauce, goat cheese, and basil to the pasta and toss well together. Serve immediately.

*Pasta with Fresh Pesto Sauce (top), Penne with Eggplant and Goat Cheese*

# Farfalle with Chicken and Sausage Sauce

**SERVES 4**

3 tablespoons olive oil

1 pound skinless boneless chicken breasts, cut in ½-inch pieces

3 Italian sausages, cut diagonally in ¼-inch slices

salt and pepper

6 scallions, cut diagonally in ¼-inch pieces

10 sun-dried tomatoes packed in oil, drained and chopped

1 cup canned crushed tomatoes

1 medium-size zucchini, cut diagonally in ¼-inch slices

¾ pound farfalle (bow-tie pasta)

**1 ▼** Heat the olive oil in a skillet. Add the chicken and sausage pieces with a little salt and pepper and cook until browned, about 10 minutes. With a slotted spoon, remove the chicken and sausage pieces from the pan, and drain on paper towels.

**2 ▲** Add the scallions and sun-dried tomato pieces to the pan and cook until softened, about 5 minutes.

**3 ▲** Stir in the canned tomatoes and cook until thickened, about 5 minutes.

**4 ▲** Add the zucchini, and return the chicken and sausage to the pan. Cook 5 minutes longer.

**5** Cook the farfalle in a large pan of boiling salted water until just tender to the bite (check package directions for timing). Drain well.

**6** Serve the pasta with the chicken and sausage sauce.

# Pasta with Spinach, Bacon, and Mushrooms

**SERVES 4**

| |
|---|
| 6 bacon slices, cut in small pieces |
| 1 shallot, finely chopped |
| ½ pound small mushrooms, quartered |
| 1 pound fresh spinach, coarse stems removed |
| ¼ teaspoon grated nutmeg |
| salt and pepper |
| ¾ pound shell-shaped pasta |
| ¼ cup freshly grated Parmesan cheese |

**1** ▼ In a frying pan, cook the bacon until it is browned and the fat is rendered. Drain the bacon on paper towels, then put it in a bowl.

**2** Add the shallot to the bacon fat in the pan and cook until softened, about 5 minutes.

**3** ▲ Add the mushrooms to the pan and cook until lightly browned, about 5 minutes, stirring frequently. With a slotted spoon, transfer the shallot and mushrooms to the bacon in the bowl. Pour off the bacon fat from the skillet.

**4** ▼ Add the spinach to the pan and cook over medium heat until wilted, stirring constantly.

**5** Sprinkle with the nutmeg. Raise the heat to high and cook briskly, stirring to evaporate excess liquid from the spinach. Transfer the spinach to a board and chop it coarsely. Return it to the pan.

**6** ▲ Return the bacon, mushrooms, and shallot to the pan and stir to mix with the spinach. Season with salt and pepper. Set aside.

**7** Cook the pasta in a large pan of boiling salted water until just tender to the bite (check package directions for timing). Just before the pasta is ready, reheat the spinach mixture.

**8** Drain the pasta well and return to the saucepan. Add the spinach mixture and toss well to mix. Sprinkle with Parmesan cheese before serving.

# Pasta with Chorizo, Corn, and Red Bell Pepper

**SERVES 4**

3 tablespoons olive oil

1 pound chorizo sausages, cut diagonally in ½-inch slices

1 onion, chopped

1 garlic clove, minced

2 red bell peppers, seeded and sliced

1½ cups fresh corn kernels (cut from 3 ears of corn) or frozen whole-kernel corn, thawed

salt and pepper

¾ pound pasta spirals (fusilli)

1 tablespoon chopped fresh basil, or ½ teaspoon dried basil

fresh basil leaves, for garnishing

**1** Heat 1 tablespoon of the oil in a skillet. Add the sausage slices and brown them on both sides.

**2** Remove the sausage from the pan with a slotted spoon and drain on paper towels.

**3** ▲ Heat the remaining oil in the pan and add the onion, garlic, and bell peppers. Cook until softened, about 5 minutes, stirring frequently.

**4** ▲ Stir the sausage and corn into the pepper mixture and heat through, about 5 minutes. Season with salt and pepper.

**5** Cook the pasta in boiling salted water until just tender to the bite (check package directions for timing). Drain well and return to the pan.

**6** Add the sausage sauce and basil to the pasta. Toss together well, garnish with basil and serve immediately.

---

# Angel Hair Pasta with Tomato-Lime Sauce

**SERVES 4**

1 pound very ripe tomatoes, peeled and chopped

1 small bunch of tender, young arugula leaves

4 garlic cloves, minced

grated rind of ½ lime

juice of 2 limes

¼ teaspoon hot pepper sauce

¾ pound angel hair pasta (capellini)

¼ cup olive oil

salt and pepper

freshly grated Parmesan cheese, for serving

**1** ▼ Combine the tomatoes, arugula, garlic, lime rind and juice, and hot pepper sauce. Stir well to mix. Set aside for 20–30 minutes.

**2** Cook the pasta in boiling salted water until just tender to the bite (check package directions for timing). Drain and return to the pan.

**3** ▲ Add the olive oil and tomato-lime sauce to the pasta. Toss well together. Season with salt and pepper. Add Parmesan cheese to taste, toss again, and serve.

*Pasta with Chorizo, Corn, and Red Bell Pepper (top), Angel Hair Pasta with Tomato-Lime Sauce*

# Macaroni and Cheese

SERVES 4

1 cup elbow macaroni

4 tablespoons butter or margarine

¼ cup flour

2½ cups milk

1½ cups shredded cheddar cheese

¼ cup finely chopped fresh parsley

salt and pepper

1 cup dry bread crumbs

½ cup freshly grated Parmesan cheese

1  Preheat the oven to 350°F. Grease a 10-inch gratin dish.

2  Cook the macaroni in a large pan of boiling salted water until just tender to the bite (check package directions for timing). Drain well.

3  Melt the butter or margarine in a saucepan. Add the flour and cook 2 minutes, stirring. Stir in the milk. Bring to a boil, stirring constantly, and simmer until thickened, about 5 minutes.

4 ▲  Remove the pan from the heat. Add the macaroni, cheddar cheese, and parsley to the sauce and mix well. Season with salt and pepper.

5  Transfer the mixture to the prepared gratin dish, spreading it out evenly with a spoon.

6 ▲  Toss together the bread crumbs and Parmesan cheese with a fork. Sprinkle over the macaroni.

7  Bake until the top is golden brown and the macaroni mixture is bubbling, 30–35 minutes.

# Noodle and Vegetable Casserole

SERVES 10

1 pound egg noodles

6 tablespoons butter or margarine

1 onion, chopped

3 garlic cloves, chopped

3 carrots, shredded

¾ pound small mushrooms, quartered

3 eggs, beaten

1½ cups large-curd cottage cheese

1 cup sour cream

2 zucchini, finely grated in a food
   processor

3 tablespoons chopped fresh basil or 1
   tablespoon dried basil

salt and pepper

fresh basil leaves, for garnishing

1  Preheat the oven to 350°F. Grease a 13- × 9-inch baking dish.

2  Cook the pasta in boiling salted water until just tender to the bite (check package directions for timing). Drain and rinse with cold water. Transfer to a mixing bowl.

3  Melt 4 tablespoons of the butter or margarine in a frying pan. Add the onion, garlic, and carrots and cook until tender, about 10 minutes, stirring frequently.

4 ▲  Stir in the mushrooms and cook 5 minutes longer. Add the vegetables to the noodles in the mixing bowl.

5  In a small bowl, combine the eggs, cottage cheese, sour cream, zucchini, basil, and salt and pepper to taste. Mix well.

6 ▲  Add the cottage cheese mixture to the noodles and mix well. Transfer to the prepared baking dish. Dot the top with the remaining butter or margarine.

7  Cover the dish with foil. Bake until the casserole is set, about 1 hour. Serve hot, in the baking dish, garnished with basil leaves.

*Macaroni and Cheese (top), Noodle and Vegetable Casserole*

# Baked Seafood Pasta

½ pound egg noodles

5 tablespoons butter or margarine

¼ cup flour

2 cups milk

½ teaspoon mustard powder

1 teaspoon fresh lemon juice

1 tablespoon tomato paste

salt and pepper

2 tablespoons minced onion

½ cup finely diced celery

¼ pound small mushrooms, sliced

½ pound cooked peeled small shrimp

½ pound lump crab meat

1 tablespoon chopped fresh dill

fresh dill sprigs, for garnishing

1  Preheat the oven to 350°F. Generously butter a 2-quart baking dish.

2  Cook the noodles in a large pan of boiling salted water until just tender to the bite (check package directions for timing). Drain well.

3 ▲  While the pasta is cooking, make a white sauce. Melt 3 tablespoons of the butter or margarine in a saucepan. Add the flour and cook 2 minutes, stirring. Stir in the milk. Bring to a boil, stirring constantly, and simmer until thickened, about 5 minutes.

4 ▲  Add the mustard, lemon juice, and tomato paste to the sauce and mix well. Season to taste with salt and pepper. Set aside.

5 ▲  Melt the remaining butter or margarine in a frying pan. Add the onion, celery, and mushrooms. Cook until softened, about 5 minutes.

6 ▲  In a mixing bowl, combine the pasta, sauce, vegetables, shrimp, crab meat, and dill. Stir well to mix.

7  Pour the mixture into the prepared baking dish. Bake until piping hot and the top is lightly browned, 30–40 minutes. Garnish with dill sprigs, if wished.

# Pasta-Stuffed Bell Peppers

## SERVES 4

6 bacon slices, chopped

1 small onion, chopped

1½ cups canned crushed tomatoes

⅛ teaspoon hot red pepper flakes

½ cup macaroni

1 cup diced mozzarella cheese

12 black olives, pitted and thinly sliced

salt and pepper

2 large red bell peppers

2 large yellow bell peppers

2 tablespoons olive oil

**1** Preheat the oven to 350°F. Grease a shallow 8-inch oval or square baking dish.

**2** ▲ In a frying pan, cook the bacon until browned and the fat is rendered. Drain the bacon on paper towels.

**3** Add the onion to the bacon fat in the pan and cook until softened, about 5 minutes. Pour off excess fat.

**4** ▲ Stir in the tomatoes and hot pepper flakes. Cook over high heat until thickened, about 10 minutes.

**5** Meanwhile, cook the pasta in a large pan of boiling salted water until just tender to the bite (check package directions for timing). Drain well.

**6** ▲ Put the pasta in a mixing bowl and add the bacon, tomato sauce, mozzarella cheese, and olives. Toss well to mix. Season to taste.

**7** Cut the stem end off each bell pepper; reserve these "lids". Remove the seeds from inside the peppers and cut out the white ribs.

**8** ▲ Divide the pasta mixture evenly among the peppers. Put on the "lids". Brush the peppers all over with the olive oil and set them in the prepared baking dish.

**9** Cover the dish with foil and bake 30 minutes. Remove the foil and bake until the peppers are tender, 25–30 minutes longer.

# Broccoli and Goat Cheese Pizza

**SERVES 2–3**

| |
|---|
| ½ pound broccoli florets |
| 2 tablespoons cornmeal |
| ½ cup tomato sauce |
| 6 cherry tomatoes, halved |
| 12 black olives, pitted |
| ¼ pound goat cheese, crumbled |
| ½ cup freshly grated Parmesan cheese |
| 1 tablespoon olive oil |
| FOR THE PIZZA DOUGH |
| 2–2¼ cups flour |
| 1 package active dry yeast (¼ ounce) |
| ⅛ teaspoon sugar |
| about ⅔ cup tepid water |
| 2 tablespoons olive oil |
| ½ teaspoon salt |

**1** For the pizza dough, combine ¾ cup of the flour, the yeast, and sugar in a food processor. With the motor running, pour in the tepid water. Turn the motor off. Add the olive oil, 1¼ cups of the remaining flour, and the salt.

**2** ▲ Process until a ball of dough is formed, adding more water, 1 teaspoon at a time, if the dough is too dry, or the remaining flour, 1 tablespoon at a time, if it is too wet.

**3** ▲ Put the dough in an oiled bowl and turn it so the ball of dough is oiled all over. Cover the bowl and let the dough rise in a warm place until doubled in bulk, about 1 hour.

**4** ▲ Meanwhile, cook the broccoli florets in boiling salted water or steam them until just tender, about 5 minutes. Drain well and set aside.

**5** Preheat the oven to 500°F. Oil a 12-inch round pizza pan and sprinkle with the cornmeal.

**6** When the dough has risen, turn out onto a lightly floured surface. Punch down the dough to deflate it, and knead it briefly.

~ COOK'S TIP ~

If more convenient, the pizza dough can be used as soon as it is made, without any rising.

**7** ▲ Roll out the dough to a 12-inch round. Lay the dough on the pizza pan and press it down evenly.

**8** ▲ Spread the tomato sauce evenly onto the pizza base, leaving a rim of dough uncovered around the edge about ½ inch wide.

**9** ▲ Arrange the broccoli florets, tomatoes, and olives on the tomato sauce and sprinkle with the cheeses. Drizzle the olive oil over the top.

**10** Bake until the cheese melts and the edge of the pizza base is puffed and browned, 10–15 minutes.

# Pita Pizzas

**SERVES 4**

4 6-inch round pita breads, split in half
horizontally

¼ cup olive oil

salt and pepper

1 small red bell pepper, seeded and
sliced

1 small yellow bell pepper, seeded and
sliced

½ pound small red potatoes, cooked
and sliced

1 tablespoon chopped fresh rosemary or
1 teaspoon dried rosemary

½ cup freshly grated Parmesan cheese

1  Preheat the oven to 350°F.

2  ▼  Place the pita rounds on a
baking sheet. Brush them on both
sides with 2 tablespoons of the oil.
Sprinkle with salt. Bake until pale
golden and crisp, about 10 minutes.

3  ▲  Heat the remaining oil in a
frying pan. Add the bell peppers and
cook until softened, about 5 minutes,
stirring frequently.

4  ▲  Add the potatoes and rosemary
to the peppers. Heat through, about 3
minutes, stirring well. Season with
salt and pepper.

5  Preheat the broiler.

6  ▲  Divide the pepper-potato
mixture among the pita rounds on the
baking sheet. Sprinkle with the
Parmesan cheese.

7  Broil about 3 inches from the heat
until golden, 3–4 minutes.

# Onion, Olive, and Anchovy Pizza

**SERVES 4**

6 tablespoons olive oil

1 pound onions, thinly sliced

3 garlic cloves, minced

1 bay leaf

2 teaspoons dried thyme

salt and pepper

2 cans anchovy fillets, drained and blotted dry on paper towels

12 olives, mixed black and green, pitted

**FOR THE PIZZA DOUGH**

1 cup whole-wheat flour

¾ cup all-purpose flour

1¼ teaspoons active dry yeast

⅛ teaspoon sugar

⅔ cup tepid water

2 tablespoons olive oil

½ teaspoon salt

**1** For the pizza dough, in a food processor combine the flours, yeast, and sugar. With the motor running, pour in the tepid water. Turn the motor off. Add the oil and salt. Process until a ball of dough is formed.

**2** Put the dough in an oiled bowl and turn it to coat with oil. Cover and let rise until doubled in bulk.

**3 ▲** Heat 3 tablespoons of the oil in a frying pan. Add the onions, garlic, and herbs. Cook over low heat until the onions are very soft and the moisture has evaporated, about 45 minutes. Season with salt and pepper.

**4** Preheat the oven to 500°F. Oil a 13- × 9-inch baking sheet.

**5 ▼** Transfer the risen dough onto a lightly floured surface. Punch down the dough to deflate it, and knead it briefly. Roll out the dough to a rectangle to fit the baking sheet. Lay the dough on the sheet and press it up to the edges of the pan.

**6** Brush the dough with 1 tablespoon olive oil. Discard the bay leaf, and spoon the onion mixture onto the dough. Spread it out evenly, leaving a ½-inch border clear around the edge.

**7 ▲** Arrange the anchovies and olives on top of the onions. Drizzle the remaining 2 tablespoons olive oil over the top.

**8** Bake the pizza until the edges are puffed and browned, 15–20 minutes.

# Pepperoni Pizza

**SERVES 2–3**

2 tablespoons cornmeal

½ cup tomato sauce

½ pound pepperoni, cut in ⅛-inch slices

2 cups shredded mozzarella cheese

Pizza Dough (page 126, Broccoli and Goat Cheese Pizza)

**1** Make the pizza dough as directed in steps 1–3 of Broccoli and Goat Cheese Pizza (page 126).

**2** Preheat the oven to 500°F. Oil a 12-inch round pizza pan and sprinkle with the cornmeal.

**3** Transfer the risen dough onto a lightly floured surface. Punch down the dough to deflate it, and knead it briefly.

**4** ▼ Roll out the dough to a 12-inch round. Lay the dough on the pizza pan and press it down evenly.

**5** ▲ Spread the tomato sauce evenly onto the pizza base, leaving a ½-inch rim of dough uncovered around the edge. Arrange the pepperoni slices on top. Sprinkle with the cheese.

**6** Bake until the cheese melts and the edge of the pizza base is puffed and browned, 10–15 minutes.

# Calzone with Bell Peppers and Eggplant

**SERVES 2**

3–4 tablespoons olive oil

½ small eggplant, cut in ½-inch-wide sticks

½ red bell pepper, seeded and sliced

½ yellow bell pepper, seeded and sliced

1 small onion, halved and sliced

1 garlic clove, minced

salt and pepper

¼ pound mozzarella cheese, chopped

Pizza Dough (page 126, Broccoli and Goat Cheese Pizza)

**1** Make the pizza dough as directed in steps 1–3 of Broccoli and Goat Cheese Pizza (page 126).

**2** Heat the olive oil in a frying pan. Add the eggplant and cook until golden, about 6–8 minutes. Add the pepper strips, onion, and garlic, with more oil if necessary. Cook, stirring occasionally, until softened, about 5 minutes longer. Season to taste.

**3** Preheat the oven to 475°F.

**4** Transfer the risen pizza dough to a lightly floured surface. Punch down the dough to deflate it, and knead it briefly. Divide the dough in half.

**5** Roll out each piece of dough into a 7-inch round. With the back of a knife, make an indentation across the center of each round to mark it into halves.

**6** ▲ Spoon half of the vegetable mixture onto one side of each dough round. Divide the cheese evenly between them.

**7** ▲ Fold the dough over to enclose the filling. Pinch the edges to seal them securely.

**8** Set the calzone on an oiled baking sheet. Bake until puffed and browned, 20–25 minutes. To serve, break or cut each calzone in half.

*Pepperoni Pizza (top), Calzone with Bell Peppers and Eggplant*

# Pizza Toasts with Eggplant and Mozzarella

**SERVES 4**

2 small eggplants, cut across in thin slices (about ½ pound)

1 tablespoon salt

½ cup olive oil

1 garlic clove, crushed with the side of a knife

8 slices French bread, ½-inch thick

½ pound mozzarella cheese, cut in 8 slices

3 tablespoons chopped fresh chives

3 tablespoons chopped fresh basil

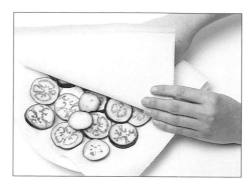

**1 ▲** Put the eggplant slices in a colander and sprinkle with the salt. Let stand at least 30 minutes to drain. Rinse the eggplant slices under cold water, then blot dry with paper towels.

**2** Heat half the olive oil in a frying pan. Add the eggplant slices and fry until golden brown, about 5 minutes on each side. Add more oil if necessary when the slices are turned over. Drain on paper towels.

**3** Preheat the oven to 325°F.

**4 ▲** In a small bowl, combine the remaining olive oil and the garlic. Brush both sides of the bread slices with the garlic oil. Place the slices on a baking sheet. Bake until golden brown, about 10 minutes.

**5** Preheat the broiler.

**6 ▲** Top each slice of garlic bread with a slice of eggplant and a slice of mozzarella. Arrange on a baking sheet.

**7** Broil about 3 inches from the heat until the cheese melts, 5–7 minutes. Sprinkle the toasts with the chopped herbs before serving.

# Mini Tomato-Phyllo Pizzas

**Serves 6**

4 large or 8 small sheets of phyllo pastry, thawed if frozen

¼ cup olive oil

1 pound tomatoes, peeled, seeded, and diced

½ cup freshly grated Parmesan cheese

½ cup crumbled feta cheese

9 black olives, pitted and halved

¼ teaspoon dried oregano

½ teaspoon fresh thyme leaves, or ⅛ teaspoon dried thyme

salt and pepper

fresh thyme or basil, for garnishing

**1** Preheat the oven to 350°F. Grease 2 baking sheets.

**2** ▲ Stack the phyllo sheets. With a sharp knife, cut into 24 6-inch rounds, using a small plate as a guide.

**4** Bake the phyllo bases until they are crisp and golden brown, about 5 minutes.

**3** ▲ Lay 3 phyllo rounds on each baking sheet. Brush the rounds lightly with olive oil. Lay another pastry round on top of each oiled round and brush it with oil. Continue layering the pastry rounds, oiling each one, to make 6 stacks of 4 rounds each.

**5** ▲ In a bowl, combine the tomatoes, cheeses, olives, and herbs. Mix well. Season with salt and pepper.

**6** ▲ Spoon the tomato mixture on top of the phyllo pastry bases, leaving the edges bare. Return to the oven to bake until heated through, about 5 minutes.

**7** Serve hot, garnished with fresh herb sprigs.

# Couscous with Vegetables

**SERVES 4**

2 tablespoons olive oil

8 small onions, peeled

1 red bell pepper, seeded and quartered

1 leek, cut across in 1-inch pieces

¼ teaspoon saffron threads

½ teaspoon turmeric

¼ teaspoon cayenne

1 teaspoon ground ginger

1 3-inch cinnamon stick

3 large carrots, cut diagonally in 1-inch pieces

1 rutabaga, peeled and cubed

2 potatoes, peeled and quartered

1 16-ounce can peeled tomatoes

3 cups chicken stock

salt and pepper

2 zucchini, cut across in 1-inch pieces

1 cup whole green beans, trimmed, about ¼ pound

1 15-ounce can chick peas (garbanzo beans), drained

2 tablespoons chopped fresh coriander (cilantro)

2 tablespoons chopped fresh parsley

FOR THE COUSCOUS

2½ cups water

½ teaspoon salt

1½ cups instant couscous

**1** Heat the oil in a large saucepan or castiron casserole. Add the onions, red bell pepper, and leek. Cook for 2–3 minutes.

~ COOK'S TIP ~

This couscous makes a filling vegetarian meal, and the recipe can be doubled or tripled. When multiplying a recipe, slightly decrease the amount of spices.

**2** ▲ Stir in the saffron, turmeric, cayenne, ginger, and cinnamon stick.

**3** ▲ Add the carrots, rutabaga, potatoes, tomatoes, and chicken stock. Season with salt. Bring to a boil. Reduce the heat to low, cover, and simmer until the vegetables are nearly tender, about 25 minutes.

**4** ▲ Meanwhile, for the couscous, put the water and salt in a saucepan and bring to a boil. Stir in the couscous. Remove the pan from the heat, cover, and set aside until all the liquid is absorbed, about 10 minutes.

**5** ▲ Stir the zucchini, green beans, and chick peas into the vegetable mixture. Simmer 5 minutes longer.

**6** ▲ Stir in the herbs and add pepper to taste.

**7** ▲ Lightly fluff the couscous grains with a fork. Pile the couscous in a mound in the middle of a shallow, round platter. Spoon the vegetables over the couscous and serve.

# Bulgur Wheat Salad

**SERVES 6**

⅔ cup fine bulgur wheat

1 cup water

1½ cups finely chopped fresh parsley

¼ cup chopped fresh mint or 2 tablespoons dried mint

¼ cup finely chopped scallions

¼ cup finely chopped red onion

1 large tomato, chopped

¼ cup olive oil

⅓ cup fresh lemon juice

salt and pepper

½ head of romaine lettuce, leaves separated

**1** Place the bulgur wheat in a bowl. Pour the water over the wheat. Let stand until the wheat swells and softens, about 30 minutes.

**2 ▲** A handful at a time, squeeze excess water out of the bulgur wheat and put it in a mixing bowl.

**3 ▲** Add the parsley, mint, scallions, red onion, and tomato to the bulgur wheat. Stir in the olive oil and lemon juice. Season to taste.

**4** Line a large serving platter with romaine leaves. Pile the bulgur wheat salad in the middle.

---

# Hot Cheesy Grits

**SERVES 6**

3 cups water

¼ teaspoon salt

¾ cup instant grits

1 egg

1½ cups shredded cheddar or Monterey Jack cheese

2 tablespoons butter or margarine

⅛ teaspoon cayenne

**1** Preheat the oven to 350°F. Grease a 13- × 9-inch baking dish.

**2** Put the water and salt in a medium saucepan and bring to a boil.

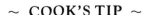

~ **COOK'S TIP** ~

Try this Southern specialty for breakfast or brunch, or in place of rice or potatoes to accompany a main course.

**3 ▲** Stir in the grits. Reduce the heat to low, cover the pan, and cook the grits until thickened, 5–7 minutes, stirring occasionally.

**4 ▲** In a small bowl, beat the egg lightly. Add a large spoonful of the cooked grits and stir well to mix.

**5** Stir the egg mixture into the remaining cooked grits in the saucepan. Add 1 cup of the cheese, the butter, and the cayenne. Stir over low heat until the cheese melts.

**6 ▲** Transfer the mixture to the prepared dish. Sprinkle the remaining cheese over the top. Bake until the cheesy grits are set and golden on top, 35–40 minutes. Let cool 5 minutes before cutting and serving.

*Bulgur Wheat Salad (top), Hot Cheesy Grits*

# Long-Grain and Wild Rice Ring

**SERVES 8**

2 tablespoons corn oil

1 large onion, chopped

2 cups processed mixed long-grain and wild rice

5 cups chicken stock

½ cup dried currants

salt

6 scallions, cut diagonally into ¼-inch pieces

parsley sprigs, for garnishing

**1** Oil a 7-cup ring mold. Set aside.

**2 ▼** Heat the oil in a large saucepan. Add the onion and cook until softened, about 5 minutes.

**3 ▲** Add the rice to the pan and stir well to coat the rice with the oil.

**4 ▲** Stir in the chicken stock and bring to a boil.

**5** Reduce the heat to low. Stir the currants into the rice mixture. Add salt to taste. Cover and simmer until the rice is tender and the stock has been absorbed, about 20 minutes.

**6** Drain the rice if necessary and transfer it to a mixing bowl. Stir in the scallions.

**7 ▲** Pack the rice mixture into the prepared mold. Unmold it onto a warmed serving platter. If you like, put parsley sprigs into the center of the ring before serving.

# Acorn Squash Risotto

**SERVES 4**

5 cups chicken stock

3 tablespoons butter or margarine

1 small onion, chopped

½ cup peeled and coarsely grated acorn squash

1½ cups arborio rice

1 zucchini, quartered lengthwise and chopped

1 cup frozen peas, thawed

½ cup freshly grated Parmesan cheese

salt and pepper

**1** In a saucepan, bring the stock to a simmer. Keep it simmering gently.

**2** Melt 1 tablespoon of the butter or margarine in a heavy saucepan. Add the onion and cook until softened, about 5 minutes.

**3** ▲ Add the grated squash to the onion. Cook 1 minute, stirring.

**4** ▲ Add the rice and stir to coat all the grains well with butter. Cook 1 minute, stirring.

**5** Add about ½ cup of the simmering stock to the rice. Cook, stirring frequently, until the stock is absorbed. Continue adding the stock, about ½ cup at a time, letting each addition be absorbed before adding the next, and stirring frequently.

**6** ▲ After about 5 minutes, stir in the zucchini pieces. After about 10 minutes, stir in the peas. The risotto will be cooked in about 20 minutes.

**7** ▲ Remove the pan from the heat. Add the remaining butter or margarine and the Parmesan and stir well. Season with salt and pepper. If you like, serve in hollowed-out cooked acorn squash halves.

# Red Beans and Rice

1 onion, chopped

1 green bell pepper, seeded and chopped

4 bacon slices, chopped

1 garlic clove, chopped

1 cup long-grain rice

2–3 teaspoons chili powder

2 teaspoons fresh thyme leaves or ½ teaspoon dried thyme

2 cups canned crushed tomatoes

1 cup chicken or beef stock

salt and pepper

1 15-ounce can red kidney beans, drained and rinsed

1 ▼ In a medium saucepan, cook the onion, green bell pepper, bacon, and garlic until the vegetables are softened and the bacon has rendered its fat, about 5 minutes.

2 ▲ Add the rice and stir until all the grains are coated with bacon fat. Stir in the chili powder and cook 1 minute.

3 ▲ Add the thyme, crushed tomatoes, and stock and stir well. Season with salt and pepper. Bring to a boil.

4 Reduce the heat to low, cover the pan, and simmer until the rice is nearly tender, about 15 minutes.

5 ▲ Stir in the kidney beans. Cover again and simmer until the rice is tender and all the stock has been absorbed, about 5 minutes longer.

6 Fluff the rice and beans with a fork, then transfer to a warmed serving dish.

# Pecan and Scallion Pilaf

**SERVES 4**

2 tablespoons butter or margarine

1 onion, finely chopped

2 cups long-grain brown rice

½ teaspoon finely grated lemon rind

2 cups chicken stock

2 cups water

¼ teaspoon salt

4 scallions, finely chopped

2 tablespoons fresh lemon juice

⅓ cup pecan halves, toasted

**1 ▲** Melt the butter or margarine in a medium saucepan. Add the onion and cook until softened, about 5 minutes.

**2 ▲** Stir in the rice and cook 1 minute, stirring.

**3 ▲** Add the lemon rind, chicken stock, water, and salt and stir well. Bring to a boil. Reduce the heat to low, cover the pan, and simmer until the rice is tender and all the liquid is absorbed, 30–35 minutes.

**4 ▼** Remove the pan from the heat and let stand 5 minutes, still covered. Stir in the scallions, lemon juice, and pecan halves. Transfer to a warmed serving dish.

# Fried Rice with Asparagus and Shrimp

**SERVES 4**

3 tablespoons corn oil

¾ pound asparagus, cut diagonally into 1-inch lengths (1½ cups)

1 cup sliced fresh shiitake mushrooms

3 cups cooked rice

1 teaspoon finely grated fresh gingerroot

½ pound cooked peeled shrimp, deveined

½ cup sliced canned water chestnuts, drained

3 tablespoons soy sauce

pepper

---

### ~ VARIATION ~

Ingredients for fried rice are infinately variable. Instead of shrimp, try scallops or cubes of firm-fleshed fish. Replace water chestnuts with a crunchy vegetable, such as snow peas.

---

**1 ▲** Heat the oil in a wok over high heat. Add the asparagus and mushrooms and stir-fry, 3–4 minutes.

**2 ▲** Stir in the rice and gingerroot. Cook, stirring, until heated through, about 3 minutes.

**3 ▲** Add the shrimp and stir-fry for 1 minute.

**4 ▲** Add the water chestnuts and soy sauce and stir-fry 1 minute longer. Season with pepper and serve.

---

# Saffron Rice

**SERVES 6**

4 tablespoons butter or margarine

⅛ teaspoon saffron threads

2½ cups long-grain rice

4 cups chicken stock

½ teaspoon salt

---

### ~ COOK'S TIP ~

If preferred, cook the saffron rice in a preheated 375°F oven, in a flameproof casserole. Bring to a boil, then transfer to the oven.

---

**1** Melt the butter or margarine in a large saucepan. Stir in the saffron.

**2 ▲** Add the rice and stir to coat all the grains well with the saffron butter.

**3 ▼** Stir in the stock and salt. Bring to a boil. Reduce the heat to low, cover, and simmer until the rice is tender and all the stock has been absorbed, about 20 minutes.

**4** Fluff the rice grains with a fork before serving.

*Fried Rice with Asparagus and Shrimp (top), Saffron Rice*

# SALADS, VEGETABLES, EGGS & CHEESE

~

*Here's a bright selection of tasty vegetable main dishes and accompaniments, colorful salads, and economical and quickly-made egg and cheese dishes, for lunch or supper.*

# Avocado, Grapefruit, and Canteloupe Salad

**SERVES 6**

1 pink grapefruit

1 white or yellow grapefruit

1 cantaloupe

2 large, ripe but firm avocados

2 tablespoons fresh lemon juice

2 tablespoons vegetable oil

1 tablespoon clear honey

¼ cup chopped fresh mint

salt and pepper

fresh mint leaves, for garnishing

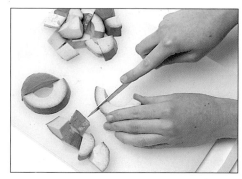

**1 ▲** Peel the grapefruit. Cut out the sections, leaving the membranes. Put the sections in a bowl.

**2** Cut the melon in half. Remove the seeds and discard them. With a melon baller, scoop out balls from the melon flesh. Add the melon balls to the grapefruit sections. Chill the fruit at least 30 minutes.

**3 ▲** Cut the avocados in half and discard the pits. Cut each half in two. Peel the skin, then cut the flesh into small pieces.

**4 ▲** Toss the avocado pieces in the lemon juice. Using a slotted spoon, transfer the avocado to the grapefruit mixture.

**5 ▲** For the dressing, whisk the oil into the reserved lemon juice. Stir in the honey, chopped mint, and salt and pepper to taste.

**6** Pour the dressing over the fruit mixture and toss gently. Garnish with mint leaves and serve immediately.

# Cool and Crunchy Salad

**SERVES 4**

1 medium red onion, thinly sliced into rings

salt and pepper

2 navel oranges, peeled and cut in sections

1 firm jícama, peeled and cut in matchstick strips

2 heads of radicchio, cored, or 1 head of red leaf lettuce, leaves separated

3 tablespoons chopped fresh parsley

3 tablespoons chopped fresh basil

1 tablespoon white wine vinegar

¼ cup walnut oil

**1 ▲** Put the onion in a colander and sprinkle with 1 teaspoon salt. Let drain 15 minutes.

**2** In a mixing bowl combine the orange sections and jícama strips.

**3** Spread out the radicchio or lettuce leaves on a large shallow bowl or serving platter.

**4 ▲** Rinse the onion and dry on paper towels. Toss it with the jícama and orange.

**5 ▼** Arrange the jícama, orange, and onion mixture on top of the radicchio leaves. Sprinkle with the parsley and basil.

**6 ▲** Combine the vinegar, oil, and salt and pepper to taste in a screwtop jar. Shake well to combine. Pour the dressing over the salad and serve immediately.

# Creamy Coleslaw

**SERVES 6**

¾ pound green or white cabbage, cut in wedges and cored

¼ pound red cabbage, cored

3 scallions, finely chopped

2 medium carrots, grated

1 teaspoon sugar

2 tablespoons fresh lemon juice

2 teaspoons distilled white vinegar

½ cup sour cream

½ cup mayonnaise

¾ teaspoon celery seeds

salt and pepper

**1 ▼** Slice the green and red cabbage thinly across the leaves.

**2** Place the cabbage in a mixing bowl and add the scallions and carrots. Toss to combine.

**3** In a small bowl, combine the sugar, lemon juice, vinegar, sour cream, mayonnaise, and celery seeds.

**4 ▲** Pour the mayonnaise dressing over the vegetables. Season with salt and pepper. Stir until well coated. Spoon into a serving bowl.

# Potato Salad

**SERVES 8**

3 pounds small new potatoes

2 tablespoons white wine vinegar

1 tablespoon Dijon-style mustard

3 tablespoons vegetable or olive oil

½ cup chopped red onion

salt and pepper

½ cup mayonnaise

2 tablespoons chopped fresh tarragon or 1½ teaspoons dried tarragon

½ cup thinly sliced celery

**1** Cook the unpeeled potatoes in boiling salted water until tender, 15–20 minutes. Drain.

**2** In a small bowl, mix together the vinegar and mustard until the mustard dissolves. Whisk in the oil.

**3 ▲** When the potatoes are cool enough to handle, slice them into a large mixing bowl.

**4 ▲** Add the onion to the potatoes and pour the dressing over them. Season, then toss gently to combine. Let stand at least 30 minutes.

**5 ▲** Mix together the mayonnaise and tarragon. Gently stir into the potatoes, along with the celery. Taste and adjust the seasoning before serving.

~ **VARIATION** ~

Substitute 3 tablespoons dry white wine for the wine vinegar, if preferred. When available, use small red potatoes to give a nice color to the salad.

*Creamy Coleslaw (top), Potato Salad*

# Caesar Salad

**SERVES 4**

2 eggs

1 garlic clove, minced

½ teaspoon salt

½ cup olive oil

juice of 1 lemon

¼ teaspoon Worcestershire sauce

1 pound romaine lettuce, torn in bite-
size pieces

½ cup freshly grated Parmesan cheese

pepper

8 canned anchovy fillets, drained and
blotted dry on paper towels
(optional)

**FOR THE CROUTONS**

1 garlic clove

¼ teaspoon salt

¼ cup olive oil

1½ cups cubed French bread

**1** Preheat the oven to 350°F.

**2** ▲ For the croûtons, crush the garlic with the salt in a mixing bowl and mix in the oil. Add the bread cubes to the bowl and toss to coat with the garlic oil.

**3** Spread the bread cubes on a baking sheet. Bake until golden brown, 20–25 minutes.

**4** Meanwhile, put the eggs in a small pan of boiling water and simmer gently for 7 minutes. Transfer the eggs to a bowl of cold water and shell them as soon as they are cool enough to handle.

**5** ▼ Mash the garlic clove with the salt in the bottom of a salad bowl. Whisk in the olive oil, lemon juice, and Worcestershire sauce.

**6** Add the lettuce to the salad bowl and toss well to coat with the dressing.

**7** Add the Parmesan cheese and season with pepper. Add the croûtons and toss well to combine.

**8** Cut the hard-cooked eggs in quarters. Arrange on top of the salad with the anchovies, if using. Serve immediately.

---

# Green Salad with Yogurt-Blue Cheese Dressing

**SERVES 6**

4 cups mixed salad leaves, such as red
leaf and Boston lettuce, torn in bite-
size pieces

1 small bunch of lamb's lettuce
(mâche), arugula, or watercress

**FOR THE DRESSING**

½ cup plain yogurt

1½ teaspoons white wine vinegar

½ teaspoon sugar

1 tablespoon fresh lemon juice

1 garlic clove, minced

¼ cup crumbled blue cheese

**1** ▼ For the dressing, combine the yogurt, wine vinegar, sugar, lemon juice, and garlic in a small bowl and mix well. Fold in the cheese. The dressing should be lumpy.

**2** ▲ Put the salad leaves in a salad bowl. Add the dressing and toss until all the leaves are coated. Serve immediately.

*Caesar Salad (top), Green Salad with Yogurt-Blue Cheese Dressing*

# Spinach and Bacon Salad

**SERVES 4**

1 hard-cooked egg

⅓ cup white wine vinegar

1 teaspoon Dijon-style mustard

2 tablespoons vegetable or olive oil

salt and pepper

1 pound fresh young spinach leaves

1 cup sliced small mushrooms

3 bacon slices

1 medium onion, chopped

2 garlic cloves, minced

**1** Separate the egg yolk and white. Chop the egg white and set aside.

**2 ▲** To make the dressing, press the egg yolk through a strainer into a bowl. Whisk in the vinegar, mustard, oil, and salt and pepper to taste.

**3** Put the spinach in a salad bowl with the mushrooms.

**4** In a small frying pan, fry the bacon until crisp. Remove the bacon with tongs and drain on paper towels.

**5 ▼** When cool, crumble the bacon over the spinach.

**6** Add the onion and garlic to the bacon fat in the frying pan and cook until softened, about 5 minutes, stirring frequently.

**7** Pour the onion and garlic over the spinach, with the bacon fat. Add the dressing and toss well to combine. Sprinkle the egg white on top and serve immediately.

# Warm Red Cabbage Salad with Spicy Sausage

**SERVES 4**

1 pound red cabbage, cut in wedges and cored

¼ cup olive oil

2 shallots, chopped

2 garlic cloves, chopped

3 tablespoons cider vinegar

¼ pound chorizo or other cooked spicy sausage, cut diagonally in ¼-inch slices

salt and pepper

2 tablespoons chopped fresh chives

2 tablespoons chopped fresh parsley

**1** Slice the cabbage wedges very thinly across the leaves.

**2 ▲** Heat the oil in a skillet. Add the shallots and garlic and cook until softened, about 4 minutes. Transfer from the pan to a salad bowl using a slotted spoon.

**3** Add the cabbage to the hot oil and cook until wilted, about 10 minutes, stirring occasionally. Add 1 tablespoon of the vinegar and cook 1 minute longer, stirring. Transfer the cabbage and the oil from the pan to the salad bowl.

**4 ▼** Add the sausage slices to the pan and fry until well browned. Transfer the sausage to the salad bowl using the slotted spoon.

**5** Pour the remaining vinegar over the salad and toss well to combine. Season with salt and pepper. Sprinkle with the chopped herbs and serve.

*Spinach and Bacon Salad (top), Warm Red Cabbage Salad with Spicy Sausage*

# Pasta and Avocado Salad

**SERVES 6**

3 cups pasta spirals (fusilli) or other small pasta shapes

½ cup drained canned whole-kernel corn or frozen whole-kernel corn, thawed

½ red bell pepper, seeded and diced

8 black olives, pitted and sliced

3 scallions, finely chopped

2 medium avocados

FOR THE DRESSING

2 sun-dried tomato halves, loose-packed (not packed in oil)

1½ tablespoons balsamic vinegar

1½ tablespoons red wine vinegar

½ garlic clove, minced

½ teaspoon salt

5 tablespoons olive oil

1 tablespoon chopped fresh basil

**1 ▼** For the dressing, drop the sun-dried tomatoes into a pan containing 1 inch of boiling water and simmer until tender, about 3 minutes. Drain and chop finely.

**2 ▲** Combine the tomatoes, vinegars, garlic, and salt in a food processor. With the machine on, add the oil in a stream. Stir in the basil.

**3** Cook the pasta in a large pan of boiling salted water until just tender to the bite (check package directions for timing). Drain well.

**4 ▲** In a large bowl, combine the pasta, corn, red bell pepper, olives, and scallions. Add the dressing and toss well together.

**5 ▲** Just before serving, peel the avocados and cut the flesh into cubes. Mix gently into the pasta salad, and serve at room temperature.

# Ham and Black-Eyed Pea Salad

**SERVES 8**

1 cup dry black-eyed peas

1 onion, peeled

1 carrot, peeled

½ pound smoked ham, diced

3 medium tomatoes, peeled, seeded, and diced (about 1 cup)

salt and pepper

**FOR THE DRESSING**

2 garlic cloves, minced

3 tablespoons olive oil

3 tablespoons red wine vinegar

2 tablespoons corn oil

1 tablespoon fresh lemon juice

1 tablespoon chopped fresh basil or 1 teaspoon dried basil

1 tablespoon whole-grain mustard

1 teaspoon soy sauce

½ teaspoon dried oregano

½ teaspoon sugar

¼ teaspoon Worcestershire sauce

½ teaspoon hot pepper sauce

**1** Soak the black-eyed peas in water to cover overnight. Drain.

**2 ▲** Put the peas in a large saucepan and add the onion and carrot. Cover with fresh cold water and bring to a boil. Lower the heat and simmer until the peas are tender, about 1 hour. Drain, reserving the onion and carrot. Transfer the peas to a salad bowl.

**3 ▼** Finely chop the onion and carrot. Toss with the peas. Stir in the ham and tomatoes.

**4** For the dressing, combine all the ingredients in a small bowl and whisk to mix.

**5 ▲** Pour the dressing over the peas. Season with salt and pepper. Toss to combine.

# Cobb Salad

**SERVES 4**

1 large head of romaine lettuce, sliced in strips across the leaves

8 bacon slices, fried until crisp and crumbled

2 large avocados, diced

6 hard-cooked eggs, chopped

2 beefsteak tomatoes, peeled, seeded, and chopped

1½ cups crumbled blue cheese

FOR THE DRESSING

1 garlic clove, minced

1 teaspoon sugar

½ tablespoon fresh lemon juice

1½ tablespoons red wine vinegar

½ cup peanut oil

salt and pepper

**1** For the dressing, combine all the ingredients in a screwtop jar and shake well.

**2 ▲** On a large rectangular or oval platter, spread out the lettuce to make a bed.

**3 ▲** Reserve the bacon, and arrange the remaining ingredients in rows, beginning with the avocados. Sprinkle the bacon on top.

**4** Pour the dressing over the salad just before serving.

---

# Spicy Corn Salad

**SERVES 4**

2 tablespoons vegetable oil

2 cups fresh corn kernels cut from the cob, or frozen whole-kernel corn, thawed

1 green bell pepper, seeded and diced

1 small fresh red chili pepper, seeded and finely diced

4 scallions, cut diagonally in ½-inch pieces

¼ cup chopped fresh parsley

½ pound cherry tomatoes, halved

salt and pepper

FOR THE DRESSING

½ teaspoon sugar

2 tablespoons white wine vinegar

½ teaspoon Dijon-style mustard

1 tablespoon chopped fresh basil or 1 teaspoon dried basil

1 tablespoon mayonnaise

¼ teaspoon hot pepper sauce

**1** Heat the oil in a skillet. Add the corn, bell pepper, chili pepper, and scallions. Cook over medium heat until softened, about 5 minutes, stirring frequently.

**2 ▲** Transfer the vegetables to a salad bowl. Stir in the parsley and tomatoes.

**3 ▲** For the dressing, combine all the ingredients in a small bowl and whisk together. Pour the dressing over the corn mixture. Season with salt and pepper. Toss well to combine, and serve.

*Cobb Salad (top), Spicy Corn Salad*

# Scalloped Potatoes

**SERVES 6–8**

2½ pounds potatoes, peeled and cut in
⅛-inch slices

salt and pepper

1 large onion, thinly sliced

¼ cup flour

4 tablespoons butter or margarine, cut
in small pieces

1½ cups shredded cheddar cheese

1 cup milk

2 cups light cream

**1** Preheat the oven to 350°F. Butter a
14-inch oval gratin dish.

**2** Layer one-quarter of the potato
slices in the prepared dish. Season
with salt and pepper.

**3** ▼ Layer one-quarter of the sliced
onion over the potatoes. Sprinkle
with 1 tablespoon of the flour and dot
with 2 tablespoons of the butter or
margarine. Sprinkle with one-quarter
of the cheese.

**4** Continue layering these
ingredients, making 4 layers.

**5** ▲ Heat the milk and light cream
in a small saucepan. Pour the mixture
evenly over the potatoes.

**6** Cover the gratin dish with foil.
Place it in the oven and bake for 1
hour. Remove the foil and bake until
the potatoes are tender and the top is
golden, 15–20 minutes longer.

# New Potatoes with Shallot Butter

**SERVES 6**

1¼ pounds small new potatoes

4 tablespoons butter or margarine

3 shallots, finely chopped

2 garlic cloves, minced

salt and pepper

1 teaspoon chopped fresh tarragon

1 teaspoon chopped fresh chives

1 teaspoon chopped fresh parsley

**1** Bring a saucepan of salted water to
a boil. Add the potatoes and cook
until just tender, 15–20 minutes.
Drain well.

**2** ▼ Melt the butter or margarine in
a skillet. Add the shallots and garlic
and cook over low heat until softened,
about 5 minutes.

**3** ▲ Add the potatoes to the skillet
and stir well to mix with the shallot
butter. Season with salt and pepper.
Cook, stirring, until the potatoes are
heated through.

**4** Transfer the potatoes to a warmed
serving bowl. Sprinkle with the
chopped herbs before serving.

*Scalloped Potatoes (top), New Potatoes with Shallot Butter*

# Mashed Potatoes with Garlic

**SERVES 6**

2–3 heads of garlic, according to taste, cloves separated

4 tablespoons butter or margarine

2½ pounds potatoes, peeled and quartered

salt and pepper

½ cup whipping cream

3 tablespoons chopped fresh chives

**1** Drop the garlic cloves into a pan of boiling water and boil 2 minutes. Drain and peel.

**2 ▲** Melt half the butter or margarine in a small saucepan over low heat. Add the peeled garlic. Cover and cook until very soft, 20–25 minutes, stirring frequently.

**3** Meanwhile, cook the potatoes in boiling salted water until tender, 15–20 minutes. Drain well and return to the pan. Set over medium heat to evaporate excess moisture, 2–3 minutes.

**4 ▲** Push the potatoes through a potato ricer or mash them with a potato masher. Return them to the saucepan and beat in the remaining butter or margarine, 1 tablespoon at a time. Season with salt and pepper.

**5 ▲** Remove the pan of garlic from the heat and mash the garlic and butter together with a fork until smooth. Stir in the cream. Return to the heat and bring just to a boil.

**6** Beat the garlic cream into the potatoes, 1 tablespoon at a time. Reheat the potatoes if necessary.

**7** Fold most of the chives into the potatoes. Transfer the potatoes to a warmed serving bowl and sprinkle the remaining chives on top.

# Candied Sweet Potatoes

**SERVES 8**

3 pounds sweet potatoes, peeled

3 tablespoons butter or margarine

½ cup maple syrup

¾ teaspoon ground ginger

1 tablespoon fresh lemon juice

**1** Preheat the oven to 375°F. Grease a large shallow baking dish.

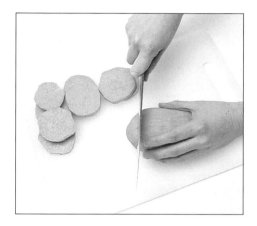

**2 ▲** Cut the potatoes in ½-inch slices. Cook them in boiling water for 10 minutes. Drain. Let cool.

**3 ▲** Melt the butter or margarine in a small saucepan over medium heat. Stir in the maple syrup until well combined. Stir in the ginger. Simmer 1 minute, then add the lemon juice.

**4 ▼** Arrange the potato slices in one layer in the prepared baking dish, overlapping them slightly.

**5 ▲** Drizzle the maple syrup mixture evenly over the potatoes. Bake until the potatoes are tender and glazed, 30–35 minutes, spooning the cooking liquid over them once or twice.

# Creamed Corn with Bell Peppers

**SERVES 4**

2 tablespoons butter or margarine

1 small red bell pepper, seeded and finely diced

1 small green bell pepper, seeded and finely diced

4 ears of corn, husks and silk removed

½ cup whipping cream

salt and pepper

**1 ▲** Melt the butter or margarine in a saucepan. Add the peppers and cook 5 minutes, stirring occasionally.

**2 ▼** Cut the kernels off the ears of corn. Scrape the cobs with the back of a knife to extract the milky liquid. Alternatively, use a corn scraper to remove the kernels and liquid.

## ~ VARIATION ~

2 cups frozen whole-kernel corn, thawed, can be substituted if fresh corn is not available.

**3 ▲** Add the corn kernels with the liquid to the saucepan. Stir in the cream. Bring to a boil and simmer until thickened and the corn is tender, 3–4 minutes. Season with salt and pepper.

---

# Fried Okra

**SERVES 6**

1½ pounds okra

½ cup yellow cornmeal

⅛ teaspoon black pepper

⅓ cup bacon drippings or corn oil

¾ teaspoon salt

## ~ COOK'S TIP ~

When removing the stems of the okra, slice through the point where it joins the vegetable. Cutting into the vegetable allows the release of the viscous insides.

**1** Wash the okra well and drain in a colander. Cut off the stems.

**2 ▲** Combine the cornmeal and pepper in a mixing bowl. Add the still damp okra and toss to coat evenly with cornmeal.

**3 ▼** Heat the bacon drippings or oil in a skillet. Add the okra and fry until tender and golden, 4–5 minutes. Drain on paper towels.

**4** Sprinkle the fried okra with the salt just before serving.

*Creamed Corn with Bell Peppers (top), Fried Okra*

# Brussels Sprouts with Chestnuts

**SERVES 6**

1 pound Brussels sprouts, trimmed

½ cup (1 stick) butter or margarine

3 celery stalks, cut diagonally in ½-inch
    pieces

1 large onion, thinly sliced

1½–2 cups canned whole chestnuts in
    brine, drained and rinsed

¼ teaspoon grated nutmeg

salt and pepper

grated rind of 1 lemon

**2 ▲** Melt the butter or margarine in
a frying pan over low heat. Add the
celery and onion and cook until
softened, about 5 minutes.

**1 ▲** Drop the Brussels sprouts into a
pan of boiling salted water and cook
3–4 minutes. Drain well.

**3 ▲** Raise the heat to medium and
add the chestnuts and Brussels sprouts
to the frying pan.

**4** Stir in the nutmeg and salt and
pepper to taste. Cook until piping
hot, about 2 minutes, stirring
frequently.

**5 ▲** Stir in the grated lemon rind.
Transfer to a warmed serving dish.

~ **VARIATION** ~

For a tasty alternative, substitute
grated orange rind for the lemon
rind, especially when serving
with pork or turkey.

# Peas and Pearl Onions

**SERVES 6**

1 tablespoon butter or margarine

12 pearl onions, peeled

1 small head of Boston lettuce, shredded

2 cups shelled fresh green peas or frozen
    peas, thawed

1 teaspoon sugar

2 tablespoons water

salt and pepper

2 sprigs fresh mint

**1** Melt the butter or margarine in a
frying pan. Add the onions and cook
over medium heat until they just
begin to color, about 10 minutes.

**2 ▼** Add the lettuce, peas, sugar,
and water. Season with salt and
pepper. Bring to a boil. Reduce the
heat to low, cover, and simmer until
the peas are tender, about 15 minutes
for fresh peas and 10 minutes for
frozen peas, stirring occasionally.

**3 ▲** Strip the mint leaves from the
stems. Chop finely with a sharp knife.
Stir the mint into the peas. Transfer
to a warmed serving dish.

*Brussels Sprouts with Chestnuts (top), Peas and Pearl Onions*

# Broccoli and Cauliflower Mold

**SERVES 6**

1–1½ pounds broccoli, stems trimmed

1–1½ pounds cauliflower, stems trimmed

FOR THE CHEESE SAUCE

3 tablespoons butter or margarine

¼ cup flour

1½ cups milk

¾ cup shredded cheddar cheese

⅛ teaspoon grated nutmeg

salt and pepper

**1** Preheat the oven to 300°F. Butter a 1-quart ovenproof bowl or round mold.

**2** Break the broccoli into florets. Drop into a pan of boiling salted water and cook 5 minutes. Drain and rinse with cold water to stop the cooking. Drain thoroughly, then spread on paper towels to dry.

**3** Break the cauliflower into florets. Drop into a pan of boiling salted water and cook 5 minutes. Drain and rinse with cold water. Drain thoroughly, then spread on paper towels to dry.

**4** ▲ Place a cluster of cauliflower on the bottom of the prepared bowl, stems pointing inwards. Add a layer of broccoli, buds against the side and stems pointing inwards. Fill the center with smaller florets.

**5** ▲ Add another layer of cauliflower florets. Finish with a layer of broccoli.

**6** Cover the mold with buttered foil. Bake until the vegetables are heated through, 10–15 minutes.

**7** Meanwhile, for the sauce, melt the butter or margarine in a saucepan. Add the flour and cook 2 minutes, stirring. Stir in the milk. Bring to a boil, stirring constantly, and simmer until thickened, about 5 minutes. Stir in the cheese. Season with the nutmeg and salt and pepper to taste. Keep the sauce warm over very low heat.

**8** ▲ Hold a warmed serving plate over the top of the bowl, turn them over together, and lift off the bowl. Serve the molded vegetables with the cheese sauce.

# Green Bean and Red Bell Pepper Stir-Fry

**SERVES 4**

1 pound green beans, cut diagonally in 1-inch pieces

2 tablespoons olive oil

1 red bell pepper, seeded and cut in matchstick strips

½ teaspoon soy sauce

1 teaspoon fresh lemon juice

**1** Drop the green beans into a pan of boiling salted water and cook 3 minutes. Drain and refresh in cold water. Blot dry with paper towels.

**2** ▼ Heat the oil in a frying pan. Add the green beans and red bell pepper and stir-fry until crisp-tender, about 2 minutes.

**3** ▲ Remove the pan from the heat and stir in the soy sauce and lemon juice. Transfer the vegetables to a warmed serving dish.

*Broccoli and Cauliflower Mold (top), Green Bean and Red Bell Pepper Stir-Fry*

# Baked Onions with Sun-Dried Tomatoes

**SERVES 4**

1 pound pearl onions, peeled

2 teaspoons chopped fresh rosemary or ¾ teaspoon dried rosemary

2 garlic cloves, chopped

1 tablespoon chopped fresh parsley

salt and pepper

½ cup sun-dried tomatoes packed in oil, drained and chopped

6 tablespoons olive oil

1 tablespoon white wine vinegar

**1** Preheat the oven to 300°F. Grease a shallow baking dish.

**2** ▼ Drop the onions into a pan of boiling water and cook 5 minutes. Drain in a colander.

**3** ▲ Spread the onions in the bottom of the prepared baking dish.

**4** ▲ Combine the rosemary, garlic, parsley, salt, and pepper and sprinkle over the onions.

**5** ▲ Scatter the tomatoes over the onions. Drizzle the olive oil and vinegar on top.

**6** Cover with a sheet of foil and bake 45 minutes, basting occasionally. Remove the foil and bake until the onions are golden, about 15 minutes longer.

# Stewed Tomatoes

**SERVES 6**

2 pounds very ripe tomatoes, stems removed

2 tablespoons butter or margarine

2 celery stalks, diced

1 small green bell pepper, seeded and diced

2 scallions, finely chopped

salt and pepper

2 tablespoons chopped fresh basil

**1** Fill a mixing bowl with boiling water and another bowl with ice water. Three or four at a time, drop the tomatoes into the boiling water and leave them 30 seconds.

**2 ▲** Remove the tomatoes with a slotted spoon and transfer to the ice water. When they are cool enough to handle, remove the tomatoes from the ice water.

**3 ▲** Peel the tomatoes and cut them into wedges.

**4 ▼** Heat the butter or margarine in a flameproof casserole or saucepan. Add the celery, green bell pepper, and scallions and cook until softened, about 5 minutes.

~ **VARIATION** ~

To make stewed tomatoes into a tomato sauce, cook uncovered in a shallow pan such as a skillet until thickened to the desired consistency.

**5 ▲** Stir in the tomatoes. Cover and cook until the tomatoes are soft but not mushy, 10–15 minutes, stirring occasionally. Season with salt and pepper.

**6** Remove the pan from the heat and stir in the basil.

# Braised Red Cabbage with Apples

**SERVES 6**

2-pound head of red cabbage, quartered and cored

salt and pepper

2 medium red onions, peeled, halved, and thinly sliced

2 Red Delicious apples, peeled, cored, halved, and thinly sliced

1½ teaspoons caraway seeds

3 tablespoons light brown sugar

3 tablespoons red wine vinegar

2 tablespoons butter or margarine, diced

**1** Preheat the oven to 400°F.

**2** Slice the cabbage quarters thinly across the leaves.

~ **VARIATION** ~

For a sharper flavor, substitute Granny Smith, Greening or other tart varieties for the Red Delicious apples in this recipe.

**3** ▲ Make a layer of one-quarter of the cabbage in a large, deep baking dish. Season with salt and pepper.

**4** ▲ Layer one-third of the sliced onions and apples on top of the cabbage. Sprinkle with some of the caraway seeds and 1 tablespoon of the brown sugar.

**5** Continue layering until all the ingredients have been used, ending with a layer of cabbage on top.

**6** ▲ Pour in the vinegar and dot the top with the butter or margarine. Cover and bake 1 hour.

**7** Remove the cover and continue baking until the cabbage is very tender and all the liquid has evaporated, about 30 minutes longer.

# Glazed Carrots and Scallions

**SERVES 6**

1 pound baby carrots, trimmed and peeled if necessary

1½ tablespoons butter or margarine

2 tablespoons honey

2 tablespoons fresh orange juice

½ pound scallions, cut diagonally into 1-inch pieces

salt and pepper

**1** Cook the carrots in boiling salted water or steam them until just tender, about 10 minutes. Drain if necessary.

**2** ▼ In a skillet, melt the butter or margarine with the honey and orange juice, stirring until the mixture is smooth and well combined.

**3** ▲ Add the carrots and scallions to the skillet. Cook over medium heat, stirring occasionally, until the vegetables are heated through and glazed, about 5 minutes. Season with salt and pepper before serving.

*Braised Red Cabbage with Apples (top), Glazed Carrots and Scallions*

# Spanish Omelet

**SERVES 4**

4 bacon slices

3 tablespoons olive oil

1 onion, thinly sliced

½ small red bell pepper, seeded and sliced

½ small green bell pepper, seeded and sliced

1 large garlic clove, minced

¾ pound small round potatoes, cooked and sliced

4 eggs

2 tablespoons light cream

salt and pepper

**1** Preheat the oven to 350°F.

**2** In a heavy 8-inch skillet with an ovenproof handle, fry the bacon until crisp. Drain on paper towels.

**3** Pour off the bacon fat from the skillet. Add 1 tablespoon oil to the pan and cook the onion and bell peppers until softened, about 5 minutes.

**4** ▲ Remove the skillet from the heat and stir in the garlic. Crumble in the bacon. Reserve the mixture in a bowl until needed.

**5** ▲ Heat the remaining oil in the skillet. Lay the potato slices in the bottom of the pan, slightly overlapping. Spoon the bacon, onion, and bell pepper mixture evenly over the potatoes.

**6** In a small bowl, beat together the eggs, cream, and salt and pepper to taste.

**7** ▲ Pour the egg mixture into the skillet. Cook over low heat until the egg is set, lifting the edge of the omelette with a knife several times to let the uncooked egg seep down.

**8** Transfer the skillet to the oven to finish cooking the omelet, 5–10 minutes longer. Serve hot or warm, cut into wedges.

# Spinach and Cheese Pie

**SERVES 8**

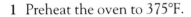

3 pounds fresh spinach, coarse stems removed

2 tablespoons olive oil

1 medium onion, finely chopped

2 tablespoons chopped fresh oregano or 1 teaspoon dried oregano

4 eggs

2 cups creamed cottage cheese

6 tablespoons freshly grated Parmesan cheese

grated nutmeg

salt and pepper

12 sheets of phyllo pastry

4 tablespoons butter or margarine, melted

**1** Preheat the oven to 375°F.

**2** ▲ Stack handfuls of spinach leaves, roll them loosely, and cut across the leaves into thin ribbons.

**3** Heat the oil in a large saucepan. Add the onion and cook until softened, about 5 minutes.

**4** Add the spinach and oregano and cook over high heat until most of liquid from the spinach evaporates, about 5 minutes, stirring frequently. Remove from the heat and let cool.

**5** Break the eggs into a bowl and beat. Stir in the cottage cheese and Parmesan cheese, and season generously with nutmeg, salt, and pepper. Stir in the spinach mixture.

**6** ▲ Brush a 13- × 9-inch baking dish with some of the butter or margarine. Arrange half of the phyllo sheets in the bottom of the dish to cover evenly and extend about 1 inch up the sides. Brush with butter.

**7** ▲ Ladle in the spinach and cheese filling. Cover with the remaining phyllo pastry, tucking under the edge neatly.

**8** Brush the top with the remaining butter. Score the top with diamond shapes using a sharp knife.

**9** Bake until the pastry is golden brown, about 30 minutes. Cut into squares and serve hot.

# Spinach Flans with Tomato-Thyme Dressing

**SERVES 6**

1½ pounds frozen chopped spinach, thawed

2 tablespoons butter or margarine

1½ cups fresh bread crumbs

salt and pepper

2 eggs

1 egg yolk

1½ cups milk

3 tablespoons freshly grated Parmesan cheese

fresh thyme sprigs, for garnishing

**FOR THE DRESSING**

5 teaspoons fresh lemon juice

1 teaspoon sugar

½ teaspoon whole-grain mustard

½ teaspoon fresh thyme leaves or ⅛ teaspoon dried thyme

½ cup olive oil

3 tomatoes, peeled, seeded, and diced

**1** Preheat the oven to 350°F. Butter 6 ramekins or custard cups. Place them in a shallow baking dish.

**2 ▲** A handful at a time, squeeze the thawed spinach to remove as much water as possible.

**3** Melt the butter or margarine in a saucepan. Stir in the spinach and cook 1 minute over high heat, stirring.

**4 ▲** Remove the pan from the heat. Stir the bread crumbs into the spinach. Season with salt and pepper.

**5** In a small bowl, beat the whole eggs with the egg yolk. Scald the milk in a small saucepan. Lightly beat it into the eggs.

**6 ▲** Add the Parmesan cheese to the milk mixture and stir into the spinach mixture.

**7 ▲** Spoon the mixture into the ramekins, dividing it evenly. Cover each ramekin tightly with foil.

**8 ▲** Add hot water to the baking dish to come halfway up the sides of the ramekins. Bake until a knife inserted in a flan comes out clean, about 35 minutes.

**9 ▲** Meanwhile, for the dressing, combine the lemon juice, sugar, mustard, and thyme in a bowl. Whisk in the olive oil. Stir in the tomatoes and salt and pepper to taste.

**10** To serve, unmold the flans onto individual plates. Spoon a little dressing over each flan and garnish with a sprig of fresh thyme.

~ **COOK'S TIP** ~

Fresh bread crumbs are easy to make using a food processor. Remove and discard the crusts from several slices of bread. Tear into smaller pieces and process to obtain fine crumbs.

# Corn and Garlic Fritters

**SERVES 4**

5 garlic cloves

3 eggs, beaten

¾ cup flour

salt and pepper

¾ cup fresh corn kernels, or drained canned corn or frozen corn, thawed

1 cup sour cream

2 tablespoons chopped fresh chives

3 tablespoons corn oil

**1** Preheat the broiler.

**2** Thread the garlic cloves onto a skewer. Broil close to the heat, turning, until charred and soft. Let cool.

**3 ▼** Peel the garlic cloves. Place them in a bowl and mash with a fork. Add the eggs, flour, and salt and pepper to taste and stir until well mixed. Stir in the corn. Set aside for at least 30 minutes.

**4** In a small bowl, combine the sour cream and chives. Cover and refrigerate.

**5 ▲** To cook the fritters, heat the oil in a frying pan. Drop in spoonfuls of the batter and fry until lightly browned on both sides, about 2 minutes, turning once. Drain on paper towels.

**6** Serve the fritters hot with the chive cream.

---

# Cheese and Mushroom Frittata

**SERVES 4**

2 tablespoons olive oil

2 cups small mushrooms, sliced

3 scallions, finely chopped

6 eggs

1 cup shredded cheddar cheese

1 tablespoon chopped fresh dill or ¼ teaspoon dried dill

salt and pepper

**1** Heat the oil in a heavy 8-inch skillet, preferably with an ovenproof handle. Add the mushrooms and scallions and cook over medium heat until wilted, about 3 minutes, stirring occasionally.

**2 ▲** Break the eggs into a bowl and beat to mix. Add the cheese, dill, and salt and pepper to taste.

**3** Preheat the broiler.

**4 ▼** Spread the vegetables evenly in the skillet. Pour the egg mixture into the skillet. Cook until the frittata is set at the edge, and the underside is golden, 5–6 minutes.

**5** Place the skillet under the broiler, about 3 inches from the heat. Broil until the top of the frittata has set and is lightly browned, 3–4 minutes. Transfer to a warmed platter for serving.

*Corn and Garlic Fritters (top), Cheese and Mushroom Frittata*

# Baked Goat Cheese with Red Bell Pepper Sauce

**SERVES 4**

¾-pound log of goat cheese, such as Montrachet, cut in 12 equal slices

1 cup dry bread crumbs

1 tablespoon chopped fresh parsley

⅓ cup freshly grated Parmesan cheese

2 eggs, beaten

fresh parsley, for garnishing

**FOR THE SAUCE**

4 tablespoons olive oil

4 garlic cloves, chopped

2 red bell peppers, seeded and chopped

1 teaspoon fresh thyme leaves

2 teaspoons tomato paste

salt and pepper

1  Preheat the oven to 450°F.

2 ▼  For the sauce, heat the olive oil in a saucepan. Add the garlic, red bell peppers, and thyme and cook until the vegetables are soft, about 10 minutes, stirring frequently.

3  Pour the pepper mixture into a food processor or blender and purée. Return the puréed mixture to the saucepan. Stir in the tomato paste and salt and pepper to taste. Set aside.

4 ▲  Place each slice of cheese between two pieces of wax paper. With the flat side of a large knife, flatten the cheese slightly.

5 ▲  In a small bowl, combine the bread crumbs, parsley, and Parmesan cheese. Pour the mixture onto a plate.

6 ▲  Dip the cheese rounds in the beaten egg, then in the bread crumb mixture, coating well on all sides. Place on an ungreased baking sheet.

7  Bake the cheese until golden, about 5 minutes. Meanwhile, gently reheat the sauce.

8  To serve, spoon some sauce on 4 heated plates. Place the baked cheese slices on top, and garnish with parsley. Pass the remaining sauce.

# Cheese and Dill Soufflés

**SERVES 6**

2 tablespoons grated Parmesan cheese

4 tablespoons butter or margarine

⅓ cup flour

1¼ cups milk

1 cup grated sharp cheddar cheese

3 eggs, separated

2 tablespoons chopped fresh dill or 1 teaspoon dried dill

salt and pepper

**1** Preheat the oven to 400°F. Butter 6 individual soufflé dishes or ramekins, and dust with the Parmesan cheese.

**2** ▲ Melt the butter or margarine in a saucepan. Add the flour and cook 2 minutes, stirring. Stir in the milk. Bring to a boil, stirring constantly, and simmer until thickened, about 5 minutes. Remove from the heat and let cool about 10 minutes.

**3** ▲ Stir the cheese, egg yolks, and dill into the sauce. Season with salt and pepper. Transfer to a bowl.

**4** In a clean mixing bowl, beat the egg whites with ⅛ teaspoon salt until stiff peaks form.

**5** ▲ Stir one-quarter of the egg whites into the cheese sauce mixture to lighten it. Fold in the remaining egg whites.

**6** ▲ Divide the mixture evenly among the prepared dishes. Bake until the soufflés are puffed and golden, 15–20 minutes. Serve immediately.

# Asparagus, Corn, and Red Bell Pepper Quiche

**SERVES 6**

| |
|---|
| ½ pound fresh asparagus, woody stalks removed |
| 2 tablespoons butter or margarine |
| 1 small onion, finely chopped |
| 1 red bell pepper, seeded and finely chopped |
| ½ cup drained canned corn or frozen corn, thawed |
| 2 eggs |
| 1 cup light cream |
| ½ cup shredded cheddar cheese |
| salt and pepper |
| FOR THE CRUST |
| 1⅔ cups flour |
| ½ teaspoon salt |
| ½ cup shortening |
| 2–3 tablespoons ice water |

**1** Preheat the oven to 400°F.

**2** For the crust, sift the flour and salt into a mixing bowl. Using a pastry blender, cut in the shortening until the mixture resembles coarse crumbs. Sprinkle in the water, 1 tablespoon at a time, tossing lightly with your fingertips or a fork until the dough will form a ball.

**3 ▲** On a lightly floured surface, roll out the dough. Use it to line a 10-inch quiche dish or loose-bottomed tart pan, easing the dough in and being careful not to stretch it. Trim off excess dough.

**4 ▲** Line the pie shell with wax paper and weigh it down with pie weights or dry beans. Bake 10 minutes. Remove the paper and weights or beans and bake until the pastry shell is set and beige in color, about 5 minutes longer. Let cool.

**5** Trim the stem ends of 8 of the asparagus spears to make them 4 inches in length. Set aside.

**6 ▲** Finely chop the asparagus trimmings and any remaining spears. Place in the bottom of the pie shell.

**7 ▲** Melt the butter or margarine in a frying pan. Add the onion and red bell pepper and cook until softened, about 5 minutes. Stir in the corn and cook 2 minutes longer.

**8** Spoon the corn mixture over the chopped asparagus in the pie shell.

**9 ▲** In a small bowl, beat the eggs with the cream. Stir in the cheese and salt and pepper to taste. Pour into the pie shell.

**10 ▲** Arrange the reserved asparagus spears like the spokes of a wheel on top of the filling.

**11** Bake until the filling is set, 25–30 minutes.

~ **VARIATION** ~

To make individual tartlets, roll out the dough and use to line 12 3-inch tartlet molds. For the filling, cut off and reserve the asparagus tips and chop the tender part of the stalks. Mix the asparagus and the cooked vegetables into the egg mixture with the cheese. Spoon the filling into the molds and bake as directed, decreasing baking time by about 8–10 minutes.

# Cheesy Bread Pudding

**SERVES 4**

3 tablespoons butter or margarine, at
    room temperature

2½ cups milk

3 eggs, beaten

½ cup freshly grated Parmesan cheese

⅛ teaspoon cayenne

salt and pepper

5 large, thick slices of crusty white bread

2 cups shredded cheddar cheese

**1** Grease an oval baking dish with the
butter or margarine.

**2** ▼ In a bowl combine the milk,
eggs, 3 tablespoons of the Parmesan
cheese, the cayenne, and salt and
pepper to taste.

**3** ▲ Cut the bread slices in half.
Arrange 5 of them in the bottom of
the prepared dish, overlapping the
slices if necessary.

**4** ▲ Sprinkle the bread with two-
thirds of the cheddar cheese. Top with
the remaining bread.

**5** Pour the egg mixture evenly over
the bread. Press the bread down gently
so that it will absorb the egg mixture.
Sprinkle the top evenly with the
remaining Parmesan and cheddar
cheeses. Let stand until the bread has
absorbed most of the egg mixture, at
least 30 minutes.

**6** Preheat the oven to 425°F.

**7** Set the baking dish in a roasting
pan. Add enough boiling water to the
pan to come halfway up the sides of
the baking dish.

**8** Place in the oven and bake 30
minutes, or until the pudding is lightly
set and browned. If the pudding
browns too quickly, before setting,
cover loosely with foil. Serve hot.

# Tomato and Basil Tartlets

**MAKES 12–18**

2 eggs

3 tablespoons whipping cream

3 tablespoons crumbled feta cheese

salt and pepper

½ pound tomatoes, peeled, seeded, and chopped

12 fresh basil leaves, cut in thin ribbons

**FOR THE CRUST**

1 ⅔ cups flour

½ teaspoon salt

½ cup shortening

2–3 tablespoons ice water

**1** Preheat the oven to 400°F.

**2** For the crust, sift the flour and salt into a mixing bowl. Using a pastry blender, cut in the shortening until the mixture resembles coarse crumbs. Sprinkle in the water, 1 tablespoon at a time, tossing lightly with your fingertips or a fork until the dough will form a ball.

**3** ▲ On a lightly floured surface, roll out the dough thinly. With a fluted 2½-inch cookie cutter, cut out 18 rounds. Use the rounds to line 18 cups in mini-muffin pans. (Muffin pans vary in size. Cut out larger rounds, if necessary, and make fewer tartlets.)

**4** In a bowl, combine the eggs and cream and beat together. Stir in the cheese and salt and pepper to taste.

**5** ▼ In a small saucepan, warm the tomatoes with the basil. Drain the tomatoes, then stir them into the egg mixture.

**6** ▲ Divide the tomato mixture evenly among the tartlet shells. Bake 10 minutes. Reduce the heat to 350°F and bake until the filling has set and the pastry is golden brown, about 10 minutes longer. Let cool on a wire rack before serving.

# BREADS, CAKES, PIES & COOKIES

~

*Both old favorites and lots of new ideas are here, for quick breads and muffins, simple cakes and layer cakes, fruit pies, nut pies, cookies and bars – all totally irresistible.*

# Corn Bread

**MAKES 9**

2 eggs, lightly beaten

1 cup buttermilk

1 cup flour

1 cup cornmeal

2 teaspoons baking powder

½ teaspoon salt

1 tablespoon sugar

1 cup shredded sharp cheddar cheese

1 cup corn kernels, cut from 2 ears of fresh corn or thawed if frozen

~ **VARIATION** ~

For a spicy cornbread, stir 2 tablespoons chopped jalapeño peppers into the batter after adding the cheese and corn.

1  Preheat the oven to 400°F. Grease a 9-inch square baking pan.

2  Combine the eggs and buttermilk in a small bowl and whisk until well combined. Set aside.

3  ▼  In another bowl, stir together the flour, cornmeal, baking powder, salt, and sugar. Pour in the egg mixture and stir with a wooden spoon until just combined. Stir in the cheese and corn.

4  ▲  Pour the batter into the prepared pan. Bake until a cake tester inserted in the center comes out clean, about 25 minutes.

5  Unmold the cornbread onto a wire rack and let cool. Cut into 3-inch squares for serving.

---

# Crunchy Corn Sticks

**MAKES 6**

1 egg

½ cup milk

1 tablespoon corn oil

1 cup cornmeal

½ cup flour

2 teaspoons baking powder

3 tablespoons sugar

~ **VARIATION** ~

Fry 3 strips of bacon until crisp. Drain, then crumble and mix into the batter before baking.

1  Preheat the oven to 375°F. Grease a castiron corn-stick mold.

2  Beat the egg in a small bowl. Stir in the milk and oil. Set aside.

3  ▼  In a mixing bowl, stir together the cornmeal, flour, baking powder, and sugar. Pour in the egg mixture and stir with a wooden spoon until just combined.

4  ▲  Spoon the batter into the prepared mold. Bake until a cake tester inserted in the center of a corn stick comes out clean, about 25 minutes. Let cool in the mold on a wire rack for 10 minutes before unmolding.

*Corn Bread (top), Crunchy Corn Sticks*

# Zucchini Bread

2 cups flour

2 teaspoons baking soda

1 teaspoon baking powder

1 teaspoon salt

1 teaspoon ground cinnamon

1 teaspoon grated nutmeg

3 eggs

1½ cups sugar

1¼ cups corn oil

1 teaspoon vanilla extract

2 cups shredded zucchini (about ½ pound)

**1** Preheat the oven to 350°F. Grease 2 5½- × 4½-inch loaf pans or a 9- × 5-inch loaf pan.

**2** ▼ Sift the flour, baking soda, baking powder, and salt in a mixing bowl. Add the cinnamon and nutmeg, and stir to blend.

**3** ▲ With an electric mixer, beat the eggs and sugar together until thick and pale. With a wooden spoon, stir in the oil, vanilla, and zucchini.

**4** ▲ Add the flour mixture and stir until just combined. Do not overmix the batter.

**5** ▲ Pour the batter into the prepared pan. Bake in the middle of the oven until a cake tester inserted in the center comes out clean, about 1 hour for 2 smaller pans or 1¼ hours for a larger pan.

**6** Let cool in the pans on a wire rack for 15 minutes, then unmold onto the wire rack to cool completely.

# Sweet Potato and Raisin Bread

**MAKES 1 LOAF**

| |
|---|
| 2½ cups flour |
| 2 teaspoons baking powder |
| ½ teaspoon salt |
| 1 teaspoon ground cinnamon |
| ½ teaspoon grated nutmeg |
| 2 cups mashed cooked sweet potatoes (about 1 pound) |
| ½ cup light brown sugar, firmly packed |
| ½ cup (1 stick) butter or margarine, melted and cooled |
| 3 eggs, beaten |
| ½ cup raisins |

**1 ▼** Preheat oven to 350°F. Grease a 9- × 5-inch loaf pan.

**2** Sift the flour, baking powder, salt, cinnamon, and nutmeg into a small bowl. Set aside.

**3 ▼** With an electric mixer, beat the mashed sweet potatoes with the brown sugar, butter or margarine, and eggs until well mixed.

**4 ▼** Add the flour mixture and the raisins. Stir with a wooden spoon until the flour is just mixed in.

**5 ▲** Transfer the batter to the prepared pan. Bake until a cake tester inserted in the center comes out clean, 1–1¼ hours.

**6** Let cool in the pan on a wire rack for 15 minutes, then unmold the bread from the pan onto the wire rack and let cool completely.

# Banana-Pecan Muffins

**MAKES 8**

1¼ cups flour

1½ teaspoons baking powder

4 tablespoons butter or margarine, at room temperature

¾ cup sugar

1 egg

1 teaspoon vanilla extract

¾ cup mashed bananas (about 3 medium bananas)

½ cup pecans, chopped

⅓ cup milk

~ **VARIATION** ~

Use an equal quantity of walnuts instead of the pecans.

**1** Preheat the oven to 375°F. Grease a muffin pan.

**2** Sift the flour and baking powder into a small bowl. Set aside.

**3** ▲ With an electric mixer, cream the butter or margarine and sugar together. Add the egg and vanilla and beat until fluffy. Mix in the banana.

**4** ▼ Add the pecans. With the mixer on low speed, beat in the flour mixture alternately with the milk.

**5** Spoon the batter into the prepared muffin cups, filling them two-thirds full. Bake until golden brown and a cake tester inserted into the center of a muffin comes out clean, 20–25 minutes.

**6** Let cool in the pan on a wire rack for 10 minutes. To loosen, run a knife gently around each muffin and unmold onto the wire rack. Let cool 10 minutes longer before serving.

---

# Blueberry-Cinnamon Muffins

**MAKES 8**

1 cup flour

1 tablespoon baking powder

⅛ teaspoon salt

⅓ cup light brown sugar, firmly packed

1 egg

¾ cup milk

3 tablespoons corn oil

2 teaspoons ground cinnamon

1 cup fresh or thawed frozen blueberries

**1** Preheat the oven to 375°F. Grease a muffin pan.

**2** With an electric mixer, beat the first 8 ingredients together until smooth.

**3** ▲ Fold in the blueberries.

**4** ▲ Spoon the batter into the muffin cups, filling them two-thirds full. Bake until a cake tester inserted in the center of a muffin comes out clean, about 25 minutes.

**5** Let cool in the pan on a wire rack for 10 minutes, then unmold the muffins onto the wire rack and allow to cool completely.

*Banana-Pecan Muffins (top), Blueberry-Cinnamon Muffins*

# Buttermilk Biscuits

**MAKES 10**

2 cups flour

1 teaspoon baking powder

½ teaspoon baking soda

1 teaspoon salt

4 tablespoons butter or margarine, chilled

¾ cup buttermilk

~ COOK'S TIP ~

If time is short, drop the biscuit dough onto the baking sheet by heaping tablespoons without kneading or cutting it out.

1 Preheat the oven to 425°F.

2 ▼ Sift the flour, baking powder, baking soda, and salt into a mixing bowl. Cut in the butter or margarine with a fork until the mixture resembles coarse crumbs.

3 ▲ Add the buttermilk and mix until well combined to a soft dough.

4 ▲ Turn the dough onto a lightly floured board and knead 30 seconds.

5 ▲ Roll out the dough to ½-inch thickness. Use a floured 2½-inch cookie cutter to cut out rounds.

6 Transfer the rounds to a baking sheet and bake until golden brown, 10–12 minutes. Serve hot.

# Parmesan Popovers

**MAKES 6**

| |
|---|
| ½ cup freshly grated Parmesan cheese |
| 1 cup flour |
| ¼ teaspoon salt |
| 2 eggs |
| 1 cup milk |
| 1 tablespoon butter or margarine, melted |

**1 ▼** Preheat the oven to 450°F. Grease six ¾-cup popover pans. Sprinkle each pan with 1 tablespoon of the grated Parmesan. Alternatively, you can use custard cups, in which case, heat them on a baking sheet in the oven, then grease and sprinkle with Parmesan just before filling.

**2** Sift the flour and salt into a small bowl. Set aside.

**3 ▲** In a mixing bowl, beat together the eggs, milk, and butter or margarine. Add the flour mixture and stir until smoothly blended.

**4 ▼** Divide the batter evenly among the pans, filling each one about half full. Bake for 15 minutes, then sprinkle the tops of the popovers with the remaining grated Parmesan cheese. Reduce the heat to 350°F and continue baking until the popovers are firm and golden brown, 20–25 minutes.

**5 ▲** Remove the popovers from the oven. To unmold, run a thin knife around the inside of each pan to loosen the popovers. Gently ease out, then transfer to a wire rack to cool.

# Devil's Food Cake

**SERVES 10**

4 1-ounce squares semisweet chocolate

1¼ cups milk

1 cup light brown sugar, firmly packed

1 egg yolk

2¼ cups cake flour

1 teaspoon baking soda

½ teaspoon salt

⅔ cup (10⅔ tablespoons) butter or margarine, at room temperature

1⅓ cups granulated sugar

3 eggs

1 teaspoon vanilla extract

FOR THE FROSTING

8 1-ounce squares semisweet chocolate

¾ cup sour cream

¼ teaspoon salt

**1** Preheat the oven to 350°F. Line 2 8- or 9-inch round cake pans with wax paper.

**2** ▲ In a heatproof bowl set over a pan of simmering water, or in a double boiler, combine the chocolate, ½ cup of the milk, the brown sugar, and egg yolk. Cook, stirring, until smooth and thickened. Let cool.

**3** ▲ Sift the flour, baking soda, and salt into a small bowl. Set aside.

**4** ▲ With an electric mixer, cream the butter or margarine with the granulated sugar until light and fluffy. Beat in the whole eggs, one at a time. Mix in the vanilla.

**5** On low speed, beat the flour mixture into the butter mixture alternately with the remaining milk, beginning and ending with flour.

**6** ▲ Pour in the chocolate mixture and mix until just combined.

**7** Divide the batter evenly between the cake pans. Bake until a cake tester inserted in the center comes out clean, 30–40 minutes.

**8** Let cool in the pans on wire racks for 10 minutes, then unmold the cakes from the pans onto the wire racks and let cool completely.

**9** ▲ For the frosting, melt the chocolate in a heatproof bowl set over a pan of hot, not boiling, water, or in the top of a double boiler. Remove the bowl from the heat and stir in the sour cream and salt. Let cool slightly.

**10** ▲ Set 1 cake layer on a serving plate and spread with one-third of the frosting. Place the second cake layer on top. Spread the remaining frosting all over the top and sides of the cake, swirling it to make a decorative finish.

# Coconut Angel Food Cake

**SERVES 10**

1½ cups confectioners' sugar

1 cup cake flour

1½ cups egg whites (about 12 egg whites)

1½ teaspoons cream of tartar

1 cup granulated sugar

¼ teaspoon salt

2 teaspoons almond extract

1 cup flaked coconut

FOR THE FROSTING

2 egg whites

½ cup granulated sugar

¼ teaspoon salt

2 tablespoons cold water

2 teaspoons almond extract

2 cups flaked coconut, toasted

**1 ▲** Preheat the oven to 350°F. Sift the confectioners' sugar and flour into a bowl. Set aside.

**2** With an electric mixer, beat the egg whites with the cream of tartar on medium speed until very thick. Turn the mixer to high speed and beat in the granulated sugar, 2 tablespoons at a time, reserving 2 tablespoons.

**3 ▲** Continue beating until stiff and glossy. Swiftly beat in the reserved 2 tablespoons of sugar, along with the salt and almond extract.

**4 ▲** Using a ¼-cup measure, sprinkle the flour mixture over the meringue, quickly folding until just combined. Fold in the flaked coconut in 2 batches.

**5 ▲** Transfer the batter to an ungreased 10-inch angel cake pan, and cut gently through the batter with a metal spatula. Bake until the top of the cake springs back when touched lightly, 30–35 minutes.

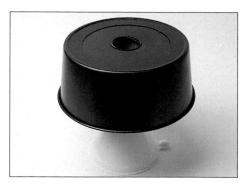

**6 ▲** As soon as the cake is done, turn the pan upside down and suspend its funnel over the neck of a funnel or bottle. Let cool, about 1 hour.

**7 ▲** For the frosting, combine the egg whites, sugar, salt, and water in a heatproof bowl. Beat with an electric mixer until blended. Set the bowl over a pan of boiling water and continue beating on medium speed until the frosting is stiff, about 3 minutes. Remove the pan from the heat and stir in the almond extract.

**8 ▲** Unmold the cake onto a serving plate. Spread the frosting gently over the top and sides of the cake. Sprinkle with the toasted coconut.

# Carrot Cake with Cream Cheese Frosting

**SERVES 10**

2 cups granulated sugar

1 cup vegetable oil

4 eggs

2 cups finely grated carrots
(about ½ pound)

2 cups flour

1½ teaspoons baking soda

1½ teaspoons baking powder

1 teaspoon ground allspice

1 teaspoon ground cinnamon

FOR THE FROSTING

2 cups confectioners' sugar

1 8-ounce package cream cheese, at
room temperature

4 tablespoons butter or margarine, at
room temperature

2 teaspoons vanilla extract

1½ cups walnut pieces or pecans,
chopped

**1** Preheat the oven to 375°F. Butter and flour 2 9-inch round cake pans.

**2 ▲** In a mixing bowl, combine the granulated sugar, vegetable oil, eggs, and carrots.

**3** Sift the dry ingredients into another bowl. Add by ½-cup measures to the carrot mixture, mixing well after each addition.

**4 ▲** Divide the batter evenly between the prepared cake pans. Bake until a cake tester inserted in the center comes out clean, 35–40 minutes.

**5** Let cool in the pans on wire racks for 10 minutes, then unmold the cakes from the pans onto the wire racks and let cool completely.

**6** For the frosting, combine everything but the nuts in a bowl and beat until smooth.

**7 ▲** To assemble, set 1 cake layer on a serving plate and spread with one-third of the frosting. Place the second cake layer on top. Spread the remaining frosting all over the top and sides of the cake, swirling it to make a decorative finish. Sprinkle the nuts around the top edge.

# Apple and Pear Skillet Cake

**SERVES 6**

| |
|---|
| 1 apple, peeled, cored, and thinly sliced |
| 1 pear, peeled, cored, and thinly sliced |
| ½ cup walnut pieces, chopped |
| 1 teaspoon ground cinnamon |
| 1 teaspoon grated nutmeg |
| 3 eggs |
| ¾ cup flour |
| 2 tablespoons light brown sugar, firmly packed |
| ¾ cup milk |
| 1 teaspoon vanilla extract |
| 4 tablespoons butter or margarine |
| confectioners' sugar, for sprinkling |

**1** ▲ Preheat the oven to 375°F. In a mixing bowl, toss together the apple slices, pear slices, walnuts, cinnamon, and nutmeg. Set aside.

**2** ▲ With an electric mixer, beat together the eggs, flour, brown sugar, milk, and vanilla.

**3** ▼ Melt the butter or margarine in a 9- or 10-inch ovenproof skillet (preferably castiron) over medium heat. Add the apple mixture. Cook until lightly caramelized, about 5 minutes, stirring occasionally.

**4** ▲ Pour the batter over the fruit and nuts. Transfer the skillet to the oven and bake until the cake is puffy and pulling away from the sides of the pan, about 30 minutes.

**5** Sprinkle the cake lightly with confectioners' sugar and serve hot.

# Ginger Cake with Spiced Whipped Cream

**SERVES 9**

1½ cups flour

2 teaspoons baking powder

½ teaspoon salt

2 teaspoons ground ginger

2 teaspoons ground cinnamon

1 teaspoon ground cloves

¼ teaspoon grated nutmeg

2 eggs

1 cup granulated sugar

1 cup whipping cream

1 teaspoon vanilla extract

confectioners' sugar, for sprinkling

FOR THE SPICED WHIPPED CREAM

¾ cup whipping cream

1 teaspoon confectioners' sugar

¼ teaspoon ground cinnamon

¼ teaspoon ground ginger

⅛ teaspoon grated nutmeg

**1** Preheat the oven to 350°F. Grease a 9-inch square baking pan.

**2** Sift the flour, baking powder, salt, ginger, cinnamon, cloves, and nutmeg into a bowl. Set aside.

**3 ▲** With an electric mixer, beat the eggs on high speed until very thick, about 5 minutes. Gradually beat in the granulated sugar.

**4 ▲** With the mixer on low speed, beat in the flour mixture alternately with the cream, beginning and ending with the flour. Stir in the vanilla.

**5 ▲** Pour the batter into the prepared pan and bake until the top springs back when touched lightly, 35–40 minutes. Let cool in the pan on a wire rack for 10 minutes.

**6 ▲** Meanwhile, to make the spiced whipped cream, combine the ingredients in a bowl and whip until the cream will hold soft peaks.

**7** Sprinkle confectioners' sugar over the hot cake, cut in 9 squares, and serve with spiced whipped cream.

# Pound Cake

**SERVES 12**

| |
|---|
| 2 cups flour |
| 1 teaspoon baking powder |
| 1 cup (2 sticks) butter or margarine, at room temperature |
| 1 cup sugar |
| grated rind of 1 lemon |
| 1 teaspoon vanilla extract |
| 4 eggs |

**1** Preheat the oven to 325°F. Grease a 9- × 5-inch loaf pan.

**2** Sift the flour and baking powder into a small bowl. Set aside.

**3** ▲ With an electric mixer, cream the butter or margarine, adding the sugar 2 tablespoons at a time, until light and fluffy. Stir in the lemon rind and vanilla.

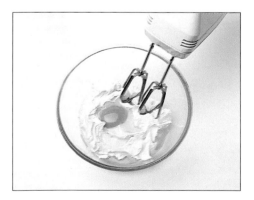

**4** ▲ Add the eggs one at a time, beating for 1 minute after each addition.

**5** ▼ Add the flour mixture and stir until just combined.

**6** ▲ Pour the batter into the pan and tap lightly. Bake until a cake tester inserted in the center comes out clean, about 1¼ hours.

**7** Let cool in the pan on a wire rack for 10 minutes, then unmold the cake from the pan onto the wire rack and let cool completely.

# Applesauce Cake

**SERVES 10**

1½ pounds apples, peeled, cored, and quartered

2¼ cups sugar

1 tablespoon water

3 cups flour

1¾ teaspoons baking soda

1 teaspoon ground cinnamon

1 teaspoon ground cloves

1¼ cups walnut pieces, chopped

1 cup raisins

1 cup (2 sticks) butter or margarine, at room temperature

1 teaspoon vanilla extract

FOR THE ICING

1 cup confectioners' sugar

¼ teaspoon vanilla extract

2–3 tablespoons milk

**1 ▲** Combine the apples, ¼ cup of the sugar, and the water in a medium saucepan and bring to a boil. Simmer 25 minutes, stirring occasionally with a wooden spoon to break up any lumps. Let cool.

~ **COOK'S TIP** ~

Be sure to grease the cake pan generously and allow this cake to become completely cold before unmolding it.

**2 ▲** Preheat the oven to 325°F. Butter and flour a 1½- to 2-quart bundt or tube pan.

**3** Sift the flour, baking soda, cinnamon, and cloves into a mixing bowl. Remove ¼ cup of the mixture to a small bowl and toss with 1 cup of the walnuts and the raisins.

**4 ▲** With an electric mixer, cream the butter or margarine and remaining sugar together until light and fluffy. Fold in the applesauce gently with a wooden spoon.

**5 ▲** Fold the flour mixture into the applesauce mixture. Stir in the vanilla and the raisin-walnut mixture.

**6** Pour the batter into the prepared pan. Bake until a cake tester inserted in the center comes out clean, about 1½ hours.

**7** Let cool in the pan on a wire rack for 20 minutes, then unmold the cake from the pan onto the wire rack and let cool completely.

**8 ▲** For the icing, put the sugar in a bowl and stir in the vanilla and 1 tablespoon of the milk. Add the remaining milk, teaspoon by teaspoon, until the icing is smooth and has a thick pouring consistency.

**9 ▲** Transfer the cooled cake to a serving plate and drizzle the icing on top. Sprinkle with the remaining nuts. Let the cake stand for 2 hours before slicing, so the icing can set.

# Pumpkin Pie

**SERVES 8**

1½ cups pumpkin purée

2 cups light cream

⅔ cup light brown sugar, firmly packed

¼ teaspoon salt

1 teaspoon ground cinnamon

½ teaspoon ground ginger

¼ teaspoon ground cloves

⅛ teaspoon grated nutmeg

2 eggs

FOR THE CRUST

1⅓ cups flour

½ teaspoon salt

½ cup shortening

2–3 tablespoons ice water

¼ cup pecans, chopped

1 Preheat the oven to 425°F.

2 ▲ For the crust, sift the flour and salt into a mixing bowl. Using a pastry blender, cut in the shortening until the mixture resembles coarse crumbs. Sprinkle in the water, 1 tablespoon at a time, tossing lightly with a fork until the dough will form a ball.

3 ▲ On a lightly floured surface, roll out the dough to ¼-inch thickness. Use it to line a 9-inch pie pan, easing the dough in and being careful not to stretch it. Trim off the excess dough.

4 ▲ If you like, use the dough trimmings to make a decorative rope edge. Cut in strips and twist together in pairs. Dampen the rim of the pie shell and press on the rope edge. Or, with your thumbs, make a fluted edge. Sprinkle the chopped pecans over the bottom of the pie shell.

5 With a whisk or an electric mixer on medium speed, beat together the pumpkin purée, cream, brown sugar, salt, spices, and eggs.

6 Pour the pumpkin mixture into the pie shell. Bake 10 minutes, then reduce the heat to 350°F and continue baking until the filling is set, about 45 minutes. Let the pie cool in the pan, set on a wire rack.

# Maple-Pecan Pie

**SERVES 8**

3 eggs, beaten

½ cup dark brown sugar, firmly packed

⅔ cup corn syrup

⅓ cup maple syrup

½ teaspoon vanilla extract

⅛ teaspoon salt

1 cup pecan halves

**FOR THE CRUST**

1⅓ cups flour

½ teaspoon salt

1 teaspoon ground cinnamon

½ cup shortening

2–3 tablespoons ice water

**1** Preheat the oven to 425°F.

**2** For the crust, sift the flour, salt, and cinnamon into a mixing bowl. Using a pastry blender, cut in the shortening until the mixture resembles coarse crumbs. Sprinkle in the water, 1 tablespoon at a time, tossing lightly with your fingertips or a fork until the dough will form a ball.

**3** On a lightly floured surface, roll out the dough to a circle 15 inches in diameter. Use it to line a 9-inch pie pan, easing in the dough and being careful not to stretch it.

**4** ▲ With your thumbs, make a fluted edge. Using a fork, prick the bottom and sides of the pie shell all over. Bake until lightly browned, 10–15 minutes. Let cool in the pan.

**5** ▼ Reduce the oven temperature to 350°F. In a bowl, stir together the eggs, sugar, corn and maple syrups, vanilla, and salt until well mixed.

**6** ▲ Sprinkle the pecans evenly over the bottom of the baked pie crust. Pour in the egg mixture. Bake until the filling is set and the pastry is golden brown, about 40 minutes. Let cool in the pan, set on a wire rack.

# Apple Pie

## SERVES 8

6 cups peeled and sliced tart apples, such as Granny Smith (about 2 pounds)

1 tablespoon fresh lemon juice

1 teaspoon vanilla extract

½ cup sugar

½ teaspoon ground cinnamon

1½ tablespoons butter or margarine

1 egg yolk

2 teaspoons whipping cream

FOR THE CRUST

2 cups flour

1 teaspoon salt

¾ cup shortening

4–5 tablespoons ice water

1 tablespoon quick-cooking tapioca

1 Preheat the oven to 450°F.

2 For the crust, sift the flour and salt into a mixing bowl. Using a pastry blender, cut in the shortening until the mixture resembles coarse crumbs.

3 ▲ Sprinkle in the water, 1 tablespoon at a time, tossing lightly with your fingertips or with a fork until the dough will form a ball.

4 ▲ Divide the dough in half and shape each half into a ball. On a lightly floured surface, roll out one of the balls to a circle about 12 inches in diameter.

5 ▲ Use it to line a 9-inch pie pan, easing the dough in and being careful not to stretch it. Trim off the excess dough and use the trimmings for decorating. Sprinkle the tapioca over the bottom of the pie shell.

6 ▲ Roll out the remaining dough to ⅛-inch thickness. With a sharp knife, cut out 8 large leaf-shapes. Cut the trimmings into small leaf shapes. Score the leaves with the back of the knife to mark veins.

7 ▲ In a bowl, toss the apples with the lemon juice, vanilla, sugar, and cinnamon. Fill the pie shell with the apple mixture and dot with the butter or margarine.

8 ▲ Arrange the large pastry leaves in a decorative pattern on top. Decorate the edge with small leaves.

9 ▲ Mix together the egg yolk and cream and brush over the leaves to glaze them.

10 Bake 10 minutes, then reduce the heat to 350°F and continue baking until the pastry is golden brown, 35–45 minutes. Let the pie cool in the pan, set on a wire rack.

# Mississippi Mud Pie

**SERVES 8**

3 1-ounce squares semisweet chocolate

4 tablespoons butter or margarine

3 tablespoons corn syrup

3 eggs, beaten

⅔ cup sugar

1 teaspoon vanilla extract

4-oz chocolate bar

2 cups whipping cream

FOR THE CRUST

1⅓ cups flour

½ teaspoon salt

½ cup shortening

2–3 tablespoons ice water

1  Preheat the oven to 425°F.

2  For the crust, sift the flour and salt into a mixing bowl. Using a pastry blender, cut in the shortening until the mixture resembles coarse crumbs. Sprinkle in the water, 1 tablespoon at a time. Toss lightly with your fingers or a fork until the dough will form a ball.

3  On a lightly floured surface, roll out the dough. Use to line an 8- or 9-inch pie pan, easing in the dough and being careful not to stretch it. With your thumbs, make a fluted edge.

4  Using a fork, prick the bottom and sides of the pie shell all over. Bake until lightly browned, 10–15 minutes. Let cool, in the pan, on a wire rack.

5  ▲  In a heatproof bowl set over a pan of simmering water, or in a double boiler, melt 3 squares of chocolate, the butter or margarine, and corn syrup. Remove the bowl from the heat and stir in the eggs, sugar, and vanilla.

6  Reduce the oven temperature to 350°F. Pour the chocolate mixture into the baked crust. Bake until the filling is set, 35–40 minutes. Let cool completely in the pan, set on a rack.

7  ▲  For the decoration, use the heat of your hands to slightly soften the chocolate bar. Draw the blade of a swivel-headed vegetable peeler along the side of the chocolate bar to shave off short, wide curls. Chill the chocolate curls until needed.

8  Before serving, lightly whip the cream until soft peaks form. Using a rubber spatula, spread the cream over the surface of the chocolate filling. Decorate with the chocolate curls.

# Banana Cream Pie

**SERVES 6**

| |
|---|
| 2 cups finely crushed gingersnaps |
| 5 tablespoons butter or margarine, melted |
| ½ teaspoon grated nutmeg or ground cinnamon |
| ¾ cup mashed ripe bananas |
| 1½ 8-ounce packages cream cheese, at room temperature |
| ¼ cup thick plain yogurt or sour cream |
| 3 tablespoons dark rum or 1 teaspoon vanilla extract |
| FOR THE TOPPING |
| 1 cup whipping cream |
| 3–4 bananas |

**1** Preheat the oven to 375°F.

**2 ▲** In a mixing bowl, combine the cookie crumbs, butter or margarine, and spice. Mix thoroughly with a wooden spoon.

**3 ▲** Press the cookie mixture into a 9-inch pie pan, building up thick sides with a neat edge. Bake 5 minutes. Let cool, in the pan, on a wire rack.

**4 ▼** With an electric mixer, beat the mashed bananas with the cream cheese. Fold in the yogurt or sour cream and rum or vanilla. Spread the filling in the crumb crust. Refrigerate at least 4 hours or overnight.

**5 ▲** For the topping, whip the cream until soft peaks form. Spread on the pie filling. Slice the bananas and arrange on top in a decorative pattern.

# Lime Meringue Pie

**SERVES 8**

| |
|---|
| 3 egg yolks |
| 1½ cups sweetened condensed milk |
| finely grated rind and juice of 4 limes |
| 7 egg whites |
| ⅛ teaspoon salt |
| squeeze of fresh lemon juice |
| ½ cup sugar |
| ½ teaspoon vanilla extract |
| FOR THE CRUST |
| 1⅓ cups flour |
| ½ teaspoon salt |
| ½ cup shortening |
| 1 egg yolk |
| 2–3 tablespoons ice water |

**1** Preheat the oven to 425°F.

**2 ▲** For the crust, sift the flour and salt into a mixing bowl. Using a pastry blender, cut in the shortening until the mixture resembles coarse crumbs. Sprinkle in the water, 1 tablespoon at a time, tossing lightly with a fork until the dough will form a ball.

~ **COOK'S TIP** ~

When beating egg whites with an electric mixer, start slowly, and increase speed after they become frothy. Turn the bowl constantly.

**3 ▲** On a lightly floured surface, roll out the dough. Use it to line a 9-inch pie pan, easing in the dough and being careful not to stretch it. With your thumbs, make a fluted edge.

**4** Using a fork, prick the bottom and sides of the pie shell all over. Bake until lightly browned, 10–15 minutes. Let cool, in the pan, on a wire rack. Reduce oven temperature to 375°F.

**5 ▲** With an electric mixer on high speed, beat the yolks and condensed milk. Stir in the lime rind and juice.

**6 ▲** In another clean bowl, beat 3 of the egg whites until stiff. Fold into lime mixture.

**7 ▲** Spread the lime filling in the pie crust. Bake 10 minutes.

**8 ▲** Meanwhile, beat the remaining egg whites with the salt and lemon juice until soft peaks form. Beat in the sugar, 1 tablespoon at a time, until stiff peaks form. Add the vanilla.

**9 ▲** Remove the pie from the oven. Using a metal spatula, spread the meringue over the lime filling, making a swirled design and covering the surface completely.

**10** Bake until the meringue is lightly browned and the pastry is golden brown, about 12 minutes longer. Let cool, in the pan, on a wire rack.

# Cherry Lattice Pie

**SERVES 8**

| |
|---|
| 4 cups sour cherries, pitted (2 pounds fresh or 2 16-ounce cans, water-pack, drained) |
| ⅓ cup sugar |
| ¼ cup flour |
| 1½ tablespoons fresh lemon juice |
| ¼ teaspoon almond extract |
| 2 tablespoons butter or margarine |
| FOR THE CRUST |
| 2 cups flour |
| 1 teaspoon salt |
| ¾ cup shortening |
| 4–5 tablespoons ice water |

**1** For the crust, sift the flour and salt into a mixing bowl. Using a pastry blender, cut in the shortening until the mixture resembles coarse crumbs.

**2 ▲** Sprinkle in the water, 1 tablespoon at a time, tossing lightly with your fingertips or a fork until the dough will form a ball.

**3** Divide the dough in half and shape each half into a ball. On a lightly floured surface, roll out one of the balls to a circle about 12 inches in diameter.

**4 ▲** Use it to line a 9-inch pie pan, easing the dough in and being careful not to stretch it. With scissors, trim off excess dough, leaving a ½-inch overhang around the pie rim.

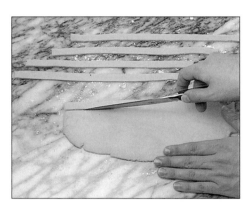

**5 ▲** Roll out the remaining dough to ⅛-inch thickness. With a sharp knife, cut out 11 strips ½ inch wide.

**6 ▲** In a mixing bowl, combine the cherries, sugar, flour, lemon juice, and almond extract. Spoon the mixture into the pie crust and dot with the butter or margarine.

**7 ▲** To make the lattice, place 5 of the pastry-dough strips evenly across the filling. Fold every other strip back. Lay the first strip across in the opposite direction. Continue in this pattern, folding back every other strip each time you add a cross strip.

**8 ▲** Trim the ends of the lattice strips even with the crust overhang. Press together so that the edge rests on the pie-pan rim. With your thumbs, flute the edge. Refrigerate 15 minutes.

**9** Preheat the oven to 425°F.

**10** Bake the pie 30 minutes, covering the edge of the crust with foil, if necessary, to prevent overbrowning. Let cool, in the pan, on a wire rack.

# Gingersnaps

**MAKES 60**

2½ cups flour

1 teaspoon baking soda

1½ teaspoons ground ginger

¼ teaspoon ground cinnamon

¼ teaspoon ground cloves

½ cup (1 stick) butter or margarine, at room temperature

1½ cups sugar

1 egg, beaten

¼ cup molasses

1 teaspoon fresh lemon juice

**1** Preheat the oven to 350°F. Grease 3–4 cookie sheets.

**2** Sift the flour, baking soda, ginger, cinnamon, and cloves into a small bowl. Set aside.

**3** With an electric mixer, cream the butter or margarine and 1 cup of the sugar together.

**4** ▲ Stir in the egg, molasses, and lemon juice. Add the flour mixture and mix in thoroughly with a wooden spoon to make a soft dough.

**5** ▲ Shape the dough into ¾-inch balls. Roll the balls in the remaining sugar and place about 2 inches apart on the prepared cookie sheets.

**6** Bake until the cookies are just firm to the touch, about 12 minutes. With a slotted spatula, transfer the cookies to a wire rack and let cool.

# Cowboy Cookies

**MAKES 60**

1 cup flour

½ teaspoon baking soda

¼ teaspoon baking powder

¼ teaspoon salt

½ cup (1 stick) butter or margarine, at room temperature

½ cup granulated sugar

½ cup light brown sugar, firmly packed

1 egg

½ teaspoon vanilla extract

1 cup rolled oats

1 cup semisweet chocolate chips

**1** Preheat the oven to 325°F. Grease 3–4 cookie sheets.

**2** Sift the flour, baking soda, baking powder, and salt into a mixing bowl. Set aside.

**3** With an electric mixer, cream the butter or margarine and sugars together. Add the egg and vanilla and beat until light and fluffy.

**4** ▲ Add the flour mixture and beat on low speed until thoroughly blended. Stir in the rolled oats and chocolate chips, mixing well with a wooden spoon. The dough should be crumbly.

**5** ▲ Drop by heaping teaspoonfuls onto the prepared cookie sheets, spacing the cookies about 1 inch apart. Bake until just firm around the edge but still soft to the touch in the center, about 15 minutes. With a slotted spatula, transfer the cookies to a wire rack and let cool.

*Gingersnaps (top), Cowboy Cookies*

# Old-Fashioned Sugar Cookies

**MAKES 36**

3 cups flour

1 teaspoon baking soda

2 teaspoons baking powder

¼ teaspoon grated nutmeg

½ cup (1 stick) butter or margarine, at room temperature

1 cup sugar

½ teaspoon vanilla extract

1 egg

½ cup milk

colored sugar, for sprinkling

**1** Sift the flour, baking soda, baking powder, and nutmeg into a small bowl. Set aside.

**2** ▲ With an electric mixer, cream the butter or margarine, sugar, and vanilla together until the mixture is light and fluffy. Add the egg and beat to mix well.

**3** ▲ Add the flour mixture alternately with the milk, stirring with a wooden spoon to make a soft dough. Wrap the dough in plastic wrap and refrigerate at least 30 minutes, or overnight.

**4** ▲ Preheat the oven to 350°F. Roll out the dough on a lightly floured surface to ⅛-inch thickness. Cut into rounds or other shapes with cookie cutters.

**5** ▲ Transfer the cookies to ungreased cookie sheets. Sprinkle each cookie with colored sugar.

**6** Bake until golden brown, 10–12 minutes. With a slotted spatula, transfer the cookies to a wire rack and let cool.

# Chocolate Chip and Macadamia Nut Cookies

**MAKES 36**

| |
|---|
| 1 cup flour |
| 1 teaspoon baking powder |
| ¼ teaspoon salt |
| 6 tablespoons butter or margarine, at room temperature |
| ½ cup granulated sugar |
| ¼ cup light brown sugar, firmly packed |
| 1 egg |
| 1 teaspoon vanilla extract |
| ¾ cup chocolate chips |
| ½ cup macadamia nuts, chopped |

**1 ▲** Preheat the oven to 350°F. Grease 2–3 cookie sheets.

**2** Sift the flour, baking powder, and salt into a small bowl. Set aside.

**3 ▲** With an electric mixer, cream the butter or margarine and sugars together. Beat in the egg and vanilla.

**4** Add the flour mixture and beat well with the mixer on low speed.

**5 ▼** Stir in the chocolate chips and ¼ cup of the macadamia nuts using a wooden spoon.

**6** Drop the mixture by teaspoons onto the prepared cookie sheets, to form ¾-inch mounds. Space the cookies 1–2 inches apart.

**7 ▲** Flatten each cookie lightly with a wet fork. Sprinkle the remaining macadamia nuts on top of the cookies and press lightly into the surface.

**8** Bake until golden brown, about 10–12 minutes. With a slotted spatula, transfer the cookies to a wire rack and let cool.

# Pepper-Spice Cookies

**MAKES 48**

1¾ cups flour

½ cup cornstarch

2 teaspoons baking powder

½ teaspoon ground cardamom

½ teaspoon ground cinnamon

½ teaspoon grated nutmeg

½ teaspoon ground ginger

½ teaspoon ground allspice

½ teaspoon salt

½ teaspoon freshly ground black pepper

1 cup (2 sticks) butter or margarine, at room temperature

½ cup light brown sugar, firmly packed

½ teaspoon vanilla extract

1 teaspoon finely grated lemon rind

¼ cup whipping cream

⅔ cup finely ground almonds

2 tablespoons confectioners' sugar

1 Preheat the oven to 350°F.

2 Sift the flour, cornstarch, baking powder, spices, salt, and pepper into a bowl. Set aside.

3 With an electric mixer, cream the butter or margarine and brown sugar together until light and fluffy. Beat in the vanilla and lemon rind.

4 ▲ With the mixer on low speed, add the flour mixture alternately with the cream, beginning and ending with flour. Stir in the ground almonds.

5 ▲ Shape the dough into ¾-inch balls. Place them on ungreased cookie sheets about 1 inch apart. Bake until the cookies are golden brown underneath, 15–20 minutes.

6 Let the cookies cool on the cookie sheets about 1 minute before transferring them to a wire rack to cool completely. Before serving, sprinkle them lightly with confectioners' sugar.

---

# Five-Layer Bars

**MAKES 24**

2 cups graham cracker crumbs

¼ cup sugar

⅛ teaspoon salt

½ cup (1 stick) butter or margarine, melted

1 cup shredded coconut

1½ cups semisweet chocolate chips

1 cup sweetened condensed milk

1 cup walnut pieces, chopped

1 Preheat the oven to 350°F.

2 ▼ In a bowl, combine the graham-cracker crumbs, sugar, salt, and butter or margarine. Press the mixture evenly over the bottom of an ungreased 13- × 9-inch baking dish.

3 ▲ Sprinkle the coconut over the crumb crust, then scatter over the chocolate chips. Pour the condensed milk evenly over the chocolate. Sprinkle the walnuts on top.

4 Bake 30 minutes. Unmold onto a wire rack and let cool, preferably overnight. When cooled, cut into bars.

*Pepper-Spice Cookies (top), Five-Layer Bars*

# Lemon Squares

**MAKES 12**

| |
|---|
| 2 cups flour |
| ½ cup confectioners' sugar |
| ¼ teaspoon salt |
| ¾ cup (1½ sticks) cold butter or margarine |
| 1 teaspoon cold water |
| FOR THE LEMON LAYER |
| 4 eggs |
| 2 cups granulated sugar |
| ¼ cup flour |
| ½ teaspoon baking powder |
| 1 teaspoon grated lemon rind |
| ¼ cup fresh lemon juice |
| confectioners' sugar, for sprinkling |

**1** Preheat the oven to 350°F.

**2** ▼ Sift the flour, confectioners' sugar, and salt into a mixing bowl. Using your fingertips or a pastry blender, rub or cut in the butter or margarine until the mixture resembles coarse crumbs. Add the water and toss lightly with a fork until the dough will form a ball.

**3** ▲ Press the dough evenly over the bottom of an ungreased 13- × 9-inch baking dish. Bake until light golden brown, 15–20 minutes. Remove from oven and let cool slightly.

**4** Meanwhile, with an electric mixer, beat together the eggs, granulated sugar, flour, baking powder, and lemon rind and juice.

**5** ▲ Pour the lemon mixture over the baked crust. Return to the oven and bake 25 minutes. Let cool, in the baking dish, on a wire rack.

**6** ▲ Before serving, sprinkle the top with confectioners' sugar. Cut into squares with a sharp knife.

# Hazelnut Brownies

**MAKES 9**

2 1-ounce squares unsweetened
   chocolate

5 tablespoons butter or margarine

1 cup sugar

7 tablespoons flour

½ teaspoon baking powder

2 eggs, beaten

½ teaspoon vanilla extract

1 cup skinned hazelnuts, roughly
   chopped

**1** Preheat the oven to 350°F. Grease
an 8-inch square baking pan.

**2 ▲** In a heatproof bowl set over a
pan of barely simmering water, or in a
double boiler, melt the chocolate and
butter or margarine. Remove the bowl
from the heat.

**3 ▲** Add the sugar, flour, baking
powder, eggs, vanilla, and ½ cup of
the hazelnuts to the melted mixture
and stir well with a wooden spoon.

**4 ▼** Pour the batter into the
prepared pan. Bake 10 minutes, then
sprinkle the reserved hazelnuts over
the top. Return to the oven and
continue baking until firm to the
touch, about 25 minutes.

**5 ▲** Let cool in the pan, set on a
wire rack for 10 minutes, then unmold
onto the rack and let cool completely.
Cut into squares for serving.

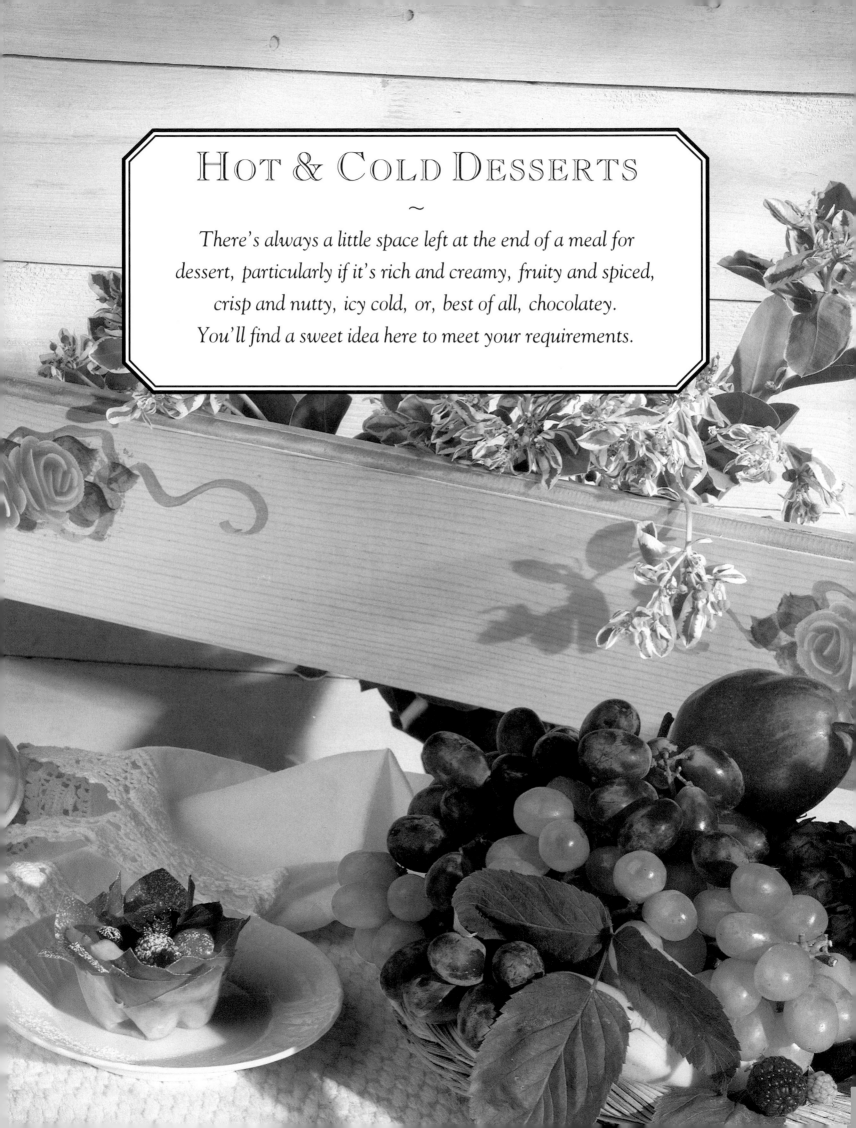

# HOT & COLD DESSERTS

~

*There's always a little space left at the end of a meal for
dessert, particularly if it's rich and creamy, fruity and spiced,
crisp and nutty, icy cold, or, best of all, chocolatey.
You'll find a sweet idea here to meet your requirements.*

# Hot Spiced Bananas

**SERVES 6**

6 ripe bananas

1 cup light brown sugar, firmly packed

1 cup unsweetened pineapple juice

½ cup dark rum

2 cinnamon sticks

12 whole cloves

**1 ▼** Preheat the oven to 350°F. Grease a 9-inch shallow baking dish.

**2 ▲** Peel the bananas and cut them into 1-inch pieces on the diagonal. Arrange the banana pieces evenly over the bottom of the prepared baking dish.

**3 ▲** In a saucepan, combine the sugar and pineapple juice. Cook over medium heat until the sugar has dissolved, stirring occasionally.

**4** Add the rum, cinnamon sticks, and cloves. Bring to a boil, then remove the pan from the heat.

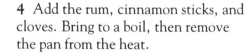

**5 ▲** Pour the pineapple-spice mixture over the bananas. Bake until the bananas are very tender and hot, 25–30 minutes. Serve hot.

# Apple-Walnut Crisp

**Serves 6**

6 cups peeled and sliced tart apples, such as Granny Smith or Greening (about 2 pounds)

grated rind of ½ lemon

1 tablespoon fresh lemon juice

½ cup light brown sugar, firmly packed

¾ cup flour

¼ teaspoon salt

¼ teaspoon grated nutmeg

½ teaspoon ground cardamom

½ teaspoon ground cinnamon

½ cup (1 stick) butter or margarine, diced

½ cup walnut pieces, chopped

**1** Preheat the oven to 350°F. Grease a 9- or 10-inch oval gratin dish or shallow baking dish.

**2 ▲** Toss the apples with the lemon rind and juice. Arrange them evenly in the bottom of the prepared dish.

**3** In a mixing bowl, combine the brown sugar, flour, salt, nutmeg, cardamom, and cinnamon. With 2 knives, or a pastry blender, cut in the butter or margarine until the mixture resembles coarse crumbs. Mix in the walnuts.

**4 ▼** With a spoon, sprinkle the walnut-spice mixture evenly over the apples. Cover with foil and bake for 30 minutes.

**5 ▲** Remove the foil and continue baking until the apples are tender and the topping is crisp, about 30 minutes longer. Serve warm.

# Baked Apples with Caramel Sauce

**Serves 6**

3 Granny Smith apples, cored but not peeled

3 Red Delicious apples, cored but not peeled

¾ cup light brown sugar, firmly packed

¾ cup water

½ teaspoon grated nutmeg

¼ teaspoon freshly ground black pepper

¼ cup walnut pieces

¼ cup golden raisins

4 tablespoons butter or margarine, diced

For the caramel sauce

1 tablespoon butter or margarine

½ cup whipping cream

**1** Preheat the oven to 375°F. Grease a baking pan just large enough to hold the apples.

**2 ▲** With a small knife, cut at an angle to enlarge the core opening at the stem-end of each apple to about 1 inch in diameter. (The opening should resemble a funnel in shape.)

**3 ▲** Arrange the apples in the prepared pan, stem-end up.

**4 ▲** In a small saucepan, combine the brown sugar, water, nutmeg, and pepper. Bring the mixture to a boil, stirring. Boil for 6 minutes.

**5 ▲** Mix together the walnuts and golden raisins. Spoon some of the walnut-raisin mixture into the opening in each apple.

**6 ▲** Top each apple with some of the diced butter or margarine.

**7 ▲** Spoon the brown sugar sauce over and around the apples. Bake, basting occasionally with the sauce, until the apples are just tender, about 50 minutes. Transfer the apples to a serving dish, reserving the brown sugar sauce in the baking dish. Keep the apples warm.

**8 ▲** For the caramel sauce, mix the butter or margarine, cream, and reserved brown sugar sauce in a saucepan. Bring to a boil, stirring occasionally, and simmer until thickened, about 2 minutes. Let the sauce cool slightly before serving.

---

### ~ VARIATION ~

Use a mixture of firm red and gold pears instead of the apples, preparing them the same way. Cook for 10 minutes longer.

# Upside-Down Pear Brownies

**SERVES 8**

½ cup flour

1 teaspoon baking powder

¼ teaspoon salt

7 1-ounce squares semisweet chocolate

½ cup (1 stick) butter or margarine

2 eggs

½ cup sugar

½ teaspoon vanilla extract

1 tablespoon strong black coffee

¼ cup semisweet chocolate chips

½ cup walnut pieces, chopped

1½ pounds ripe pears, or 2 14-ounce cans pear quarters, drained

**1** Preheat the oven to 375°F. Grease a 9-inch round nonstick baking dish.

**2** Sift the flour, baking powder, and salt into a small bowl. Set aside.

**3** In a heatproof bowl set over a pan of simmering water, or in a double boiler, melt the chocolate and butter or margarine. Remove the bowl from the heat and let cool slightly.

**4** ▲ Beat the eggs, sugar, vanilla, and coffee into the melted chocolate mixture. Stir in the flour mixture, chocolate chips, and walnuts.

**5** ▲ If using fresh pears, peel, quarter, and core them. Arrange the pear quarters in the prepared baking dish, with the rounded ends against the side of the dish. Pour the batter evenly over the pears.

**6** Bake 1 hour, covering with foil after 30 minutes. Let cool 15 minutes, then hold an upturned plate tightly over the top of the baking dish, invert and unmold. Serve hot.

---

# Ginger Baked Pears

**SERVES 6**

6 large firm pears, peeled, cored, and sliced lengthwise

¼ cup honey

¼ cup light brown sugar, firmly packed

1 tablespoon finely grated fresh gingerroot

½ cup whipping cream

~ **VARIATION** ~

Substitute firm (even underripe) peaches for the pears. To peel, dip the peaches in boiling water for about a minute, then slip off the skins. Cook as for pears.

**1** ▼ Preheat the oven to 400°F. Butter a 10-inch oval gratin dish or shallow baking dish. Fan the pear slices in a spiral design in the bottom of the baking dish.

**2** ▲ In a small bowl, mix together the honey, brown sugar, gingerroot, and cream. Pour this mixture over the pears.

**3** Bake until the pears are tender and the top is lightly golden, about 30 minutes. Serve hot.

*Upside-Down Pear Brownies (top), Ginger Baked Pears*

# Blueberry Buckle

**SERVES 8**

2 cups flour

2 teaspoons baking powder

½ teaspoon salt

½ cup (1 stick) butter or margarine, at room temperature

¾ cup granulated sugar

1 egg

½ teaspoon vanilla extract

¾ cup milk

1 pint fresh blueberries

whipped cream, for serving

**FOR THE TOPPING**

½ cup light brown sugar, firmly packed

½ cup flour

½ teaspoon salt

½ teaspoon ground allspice

4 tablespoons butter or margarine

2 teaspoons milk

1 teaspoon vanilla extract

**1** Preheat the oven to 375°F. Grease a 9-inch round gratin dish or shallow baking dish.

**2** Sift the flour, baking powder, and salt into a small bowl. Set aside.

**3** ▲ With an electric mixer, or using a wooden spoon, cream together the butter or margarine and granulated sugar. Beat in the egg and vanilla. Add the flour mixture alternately with the milk, beginning and ending with the flour.

**4** ▲ Pour the batter into the prepared dish. Sprinkle the blueberries evenly over the batter.

**5** ▲ For the topping, combine the brown sugar, flour, salt, and allspice in a bowl. With a pastry blender, cut in the butter or margarine until the mixture resembles coarse crumbs.

**6** ▲ Mix together the milk and vanilla. Drizzle over the flour mixture and toss lightly with a fork to mix.

**7** Sprinkle the topping over the blueberries. Bake until a cake tester inserted in the center comes out clean, about 45 minutes. Serve warm, with whipped cream if you like.

# Peach Cobbler

**SERVES 6**

5 cups peeled and sliced peaches (about 3 pounds)

3 tablespoons sugar

2 tablespoons peach brandy

1 tablespoon fresh lemon juice

1 tablespoon cornstarch

FOR THE DOUGH

1 cup flour

1½ teaspoons baking powder

¼ teaspoon salt

⅓ cup finely ground almonds

¼ cup plus 1 tablespoon sugar

4 tablespoons butter or margarine

⅓ cup milk

¼ teaspoon almond extract

**1** Preheat the oven to 425°F.

**2** In a bowl, toss the peaches with the sugar, peach brandy, lemon juice, and cornstarch.

**3** Spoon the peach mixture into a 2-quart baking dish.

**4 ▲** For the dough, sift the flour, baking powder, and salt into a mixing bowl. Stir in the ground almonds and ¼ cup sugar. With 2 knives, or a pastry blender, cut in the butter or margarine until the mixture resembles coarse crumbs.

**5 ▼** Add the milk and almond extract and stir until the dough is just combined.

**6 ▲** Drop the dough by spoonfuls onto the peaches. Sprinkle with the remaining tablespoon of sugar.

**7** Bake until the cobbler topping is browned, 30–35 minutes. Serve hot, with ice cream, if you like.

# Indian Pudding

**SERVES 6**

4 cups milk

¼ cup cornmeal

½ teaspoon salt

¼ teaspoon ground ginger

¾ teaspoon ground cinnamon

4 tablespoons butter or margarine

¾ cup light molasses

2 eggs, beaten

**1** Heat 3 cups of the milk in a saucepan.

**2** In a heatproof bowl set over a pan of boiling water, or in a double boiler, combine the cornmeal, salt, ginger, cinnamon, and remaining milk.

**3** ▼ Pour in the heated milk, stirring to combine. Cook, stirring constantly, until smooth.

**4** Reduce the heat so the water is just simmering, and cook 25 minutes, stirring frequently.

**5** Preheat the oven to 350°F. Grease a deep 1-quart earthenware or porcelain baking dish.

**6** ▲ Remove the bowl from the heat. Stir in the butter or margarine and molasses until the mixture is smooth. Stir in the eggs.

**7** Pour the batter into the prepared baking dish. Bake 1 hour. Serve warm.

# Lemon Sponge Pudding

**SERVES 6**

1 cup flour

1 teaspoon baking powder

¼ + ⅛ teaspoon salt

½ cup (1 stick) butter or margarine, at room temperature

1⅓ cups sugar

finely grated rind and juice of 4 large lemons

4 eggs, separated

1¼ cups milk

**1** Preheat the oven to 350°F. Butter a 10-inch shallow oval baking dish.

**2** Sift the flour, baking powder, and ¼ teaspoon salt into a small bowl. Set aside.

**3** ▼ With an electric mixer, beat together the butter or margarine, sugar, and lemon rind. Beat in the egg yolks, one at a time. Mix in the flour mixture alternately with the milk and lemon juice (reserving a squeeze of juice), beginning and ending with the flour.

**4** ▲ In a clean bowl, beat the egg whites with the ⅛ teaspoon salt and squeeze of lemon juice until stiff peaks form. Fold into the lemon batter.

**5** Pour into the prepared baking dish. Bake until golden brown, 40–45 minutes. Serve hot.

*Indian Pudding (top), Lemon Sponge Pudding*

# Bread Pudding with Bourbon Sauce

**SERVES 8**

3 cups stale French bread, in ¾-inch cubes (about 6 ounces)

2 cups milk

2 eggs

1 cup sugar

1 tablespoon vanilla extract

½ teaspoon ground cinnamon

¼ teaspoon grated nutmeg

4 tablespoons butter or margarine, melted and cooled slightly

½ cup raisins

FOR THE SAUCE

2 egg yolks

½ cup (1 stick) butter or margarine

1 cup sugar

⅓ cup bourbon whiskey

**1** ▲ Preheat the oven to 350°F. Grease an 8-inch baking dish.

**2** ▲ Put the bread cubes in a bowl with the milk and squeeze the bread with your hands until well saturated.

**3** ▲ With an electric mixer on high speed, beat the eggs with the sugar until pale and thick. Stir in the vanilla, cinnamon, nutmeg, butter or margarine, and raisins.

**4** ▲ Add the soaked bread cube mixture and stir well to mix. Let stand 10 minutes.

**5** ▲ Transfer the mixture to the prepared baking dish. Bake until firm and a knife inserted in the middle comes out clean, 45–50 minutes. Let it cool slightly in the dish, set on a wire rack.

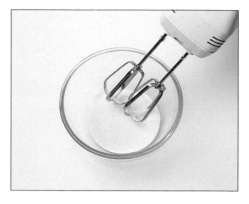

**6** ▲ Meanwhile, make the sauce. With an electric mixer, beat the egg yolks until thick and pale.

**7** ▲ Melt the butter or margarine and sugar in a saucepan. Pour the butter-sugar mixture over the egg yolks, beating constantly, until well thickened. Stir in the whiskey.

**8** Serve the warm pudding from its baking dish. Pass the hot whiskey sauce separately.

~ COOK'S TIP ~

It is important to allow enough time for the egg mixture to soak the bread thoroughly; otherwise the bread cubes will float on top, leaving a layer of custard on the bottom when the dish is cooked.

# Chocolate Pudding Cake

**SERVES 6**

¾ cup flour

2 teaspoons baking powder

⅛ teaspoon salt

4 tablespoons butter or margarine

1 1-ounce square unsweetened chocolate

½ cup granulated sugar

6 tablespoons milk

¼ teaspoon vanilla extract

whipped cream, for serving

**FOR THE TOPPING**

2 tablespoons instant coffee

1¼ cups hot water

½ cup dark brown sugar, firmly packed

⅓ cup granulated sugar

2 tablespoons unsweetened cocoa powder

**1** Preheat the oven to 350°F. Grease a 9-inch square baking pan.

**2** Sift the flour, baking powder, and salt into a small bowl. Set aside.

**3** In a heatproof bowl set over simmering water, or in a double boiler, melt the butter or margarine, chocolate, and granulated sugar, stirring occasionally. Remove the bowl from the heat.

**4** ▲ Add the flour mixture and stir well. Stir in the milk and vanilla.

**5** ▲ Pour the batter into the prepared baking pan.

**6** For the topping, dissolve the coffee in the water. Let cool.

**7** ▲ Mix together the sugars and cocoa powder. Sprinkle the mixture over the batter.

**8** ▲ Pour the coffee evenly over the surface. Bake 40 minutes. Serve immediately with whipped cream.

# Individual Chocolate Soufflés

**SERVES 6**

5 tablespoons sugar

½ cup plus 1 tablespoon unsweetened cocoa powder

⅓ cup cold water

6 egg whites

confectioners' sugar, for dusting

**1** Preheat the oven to 375°F. Lightly butter 6 individual soufflé dishes or ramekins. Mix together 1 tablespoon of sugar and 1 tablespoon of cocoa powder. Sprinkle this mixture over the bottom and sides of the dishes and shake out any excess.

**2** ▲ In a saucepan, combine the remaining cocoa powder and the cold water. Bring to a boil over medium heat, whisking constantly. Pour into a mixing bowl.

**3** ▲ With an electric mixer, beat the egg whites until soft peaks form. Add the remaining sugar and continue beating until the peaks are stiff.

**4** ▼ Add one-quarter of the egg whites to the chocolate mixture and stir well to combine. Add the remaining egg whites and fold gently but thoroughly, until no streaks of white are visible.

**5** ▲ Divide the chocolate mixture between the prepared dishes, filling them to the top. Smooth the surface with a metal spatula. Run your thumb around the rim of each dish so the mixture will not stick when rising.

**6** Bake until well risen and set, 14–16 minutes. Dust with confectioners' sugar and serve immediately.

# Fruit Kabobs with Mango-Yogurt Sauce

**SERVES 4**

½ pineapple, peeled, cored, and cubed

2 kiwis, peeled and cubed

½ pint strawberries, hulled and cut in half lengthwise, if large

½ mango, peeled, pitted, and cubed

FOR THE SAUCE

½ cup fresh mango purée, from 1–1½ peeled and pitted mangoes

½ cup thick plain yogurt

1 teaspoon sugar

⅛ teaspoon vanilla extract

1 tablespoon finely shredded fresh mint leaves

**1** To make the sauce, beat together the mango purée, yogurt, sugar, and vanilla with an electric mixer.

**2** ▼ Stir in the mint. Cover the sauce and refrigerate until required.

**3** ▲ Thread the fruit onto 12 6-inch wooden skewers, alternating the pineapple, kiwis, strawberries, and mango cubes.

**4** Arrange the kabobs on a large serving tray with the mango-yogurt sauce in the center.

# Tropical Fruits in Cinnamon Syrup

**SERVES 6**

2 cups sugar

1 cinnamon stick

1 large or 2 medium papayas (about 1½ pounds), peeled, seeded, and cut lengthwise into thin pieces

1 large or 2 medium mangoes (about 1½ pounds), peeled, pitted, and cut lengthwise into thin pieces

1 large or 2 small starfruit (about ½ pound), thinly sliced

**1** Sprinkle ⅔ cup of the sugar over the bottom of a large saucepan. Add the cinnamon stick and half the papaya, mango, and starfruit pieces.

~ **COOK'S TIP** ~

Starfruit is sometimes called carambola.

**2** ▼ Sprinkle ⅔ cup of the remaining sugar over the fruit pieces in the pan. Add the remaining fruit and sprinkle with the remaining ⅔ cup sugar.

**3** Cover the pan and cook the fruit over medium-low heat until the sugar dissolves completely, 35–45 minutes. Shake the pan occasionally, but do not stir or the fruit will collapse.

**4** ▲ Uncover the pan and simmer until the fruit begins to appear translucent, about 10 minutes. Remove the pan from the heat and let stand to cool.

**5** Transfer the fruit and syrup to a bowl, cover, and refrigerate overnight.

*Fruit Kabobs with Mango-Yogurt Sauce (top), Tropical Fruits in Cinnamon Syrup*

# Rice Pudding with Mixed Berry Sauce

**SERVES 6**

| |
|---|
| 2 cups short-grain rice |
| 1⅓ cups milk |
| ⅛ teaspoon salt |
| ½ cup light brown sugar, firmly packed |
| 1 teaspoon vanilla extract |
| 2 eggs, beaten |
| grated rind of 1 lemon |
| 1 teaspoon fresh lemon juice |
| 2 tablespoons butter or margarine |
| FOR THE SAUCE |
| ½ pint strawberries, hulled and quartered |
| ½ pint raspberries |
| ½ cup granulated sugar |
| grated rind of 1 lemon |

**1** Preheat the oven to 325°F. Grease a deep 2-quart baking dish.

**2 ▼** Bring a medium saucepan of water to a boil. Add the rice and boil 5 minutes. Drain. Transfer the rice to the prepared baking dish.

**3** In a medium bowl, combine the milk, salt, brown sugar, vanilla, eggs, and lemon rind and juice. Pour this mixture over the rice and stir well.

**4 ▲** Dot the surface of the rice mixture with the butter or margarine. Bake until the rice is cooked and creamy, about 50 minutes.

**5 ▲** Meanwhile, for the sauce, combine the berries and sugar in a small saucepan. Stir over low heat until the sugar dissolves completely and the fruit is becoming pulpy. Transfer to a bowl and stir in the lemon rind. Refrigerate until required.

**6 ▲** Remove the rice pudding from the oven. Let cool completely, and serve with the berry sauce.

# Phyllo Fruit Baskets

**SERVES 6**

| |
|---|
| 4 large or 8 small sheets of phyllo pastry, thawed if frozen |
| 5 tablespoons butter or margarine, melted |
| 1 cup whipping cream |
| ¼ cup strawberry preserves |
| 1 tablespoon Cointreau or other orange liqueur |
| 1 cup seedless red grapes, halved |
| 1 cup seedless green grapes, halved |
| 1 cup fresh pineapple cubes |
| ½ pint raspberries |
| 2 tablespoons confectioners' sugar |
| 6 small sprigs of fresh mint, for garnishing |

**1** Preheat the oven to 350°F. Grease 6 cups of a muffin pan.

**2** ▲ Stack the phyllo sheets and cut with a sharp knife or scissors into 24 4½-inch squares.

**3** ▲ Lay 4 squares of pastry in each of the 6 muffin cups. Press the pastry firmly into the cups, rotating slightly to make star-shaped baskets.

**4** ▼ Brush the pastry baskets lightly with butter or margarine. Bake until the pastry is crisp and golden, 5–7 minutes. Let cool on a wire rack.

**5** In a bowl, lightly whip the cream until soft peaks form. Gently fold the strawberry preserves and Cointreau into the cream.

**6** ▲ Just before serving, spoon a little of the cream mixture into each pastry basket. Top with the fruit. Sprinkle with confectioners' sugar and decorate each basket with a small sprig of mint.

# Strawberry Shortcake

**SERVES 6**

1½ pints strawberries, hulled and halved or quartered, depending on size

3 tablespoons confectioners' sugar

1 cup whipping cream

mint leaves, for garnishing

FOR THE BISCUITS

2 cups flour

6 tablespoons granulated sugar

1 tablespoon baking powder

½ teaspoon salt

1 cup whipping cream

**1** Preheat the oven to 400°F. Lightly grease a baking sheet.

**2 ▲** For the biscuits, sift the flour into a mixing bowl. Add 4 tablespoons of the granulated sugar, the baking powder, and salt. Stir well.

**3 ▲** Gradually add the cream, tossing lightly with a fork until the mixture forms clumps.

**4 ▲** Gather the clumps together, but do not knead the dough. Shape the dough into a 6-inch log. Cut into 6 slices and place them on the prepared baking sheet.

**5 ▲** Sprinkle with the remaining 2 tablespoons granulated sugar. Bake until light golden brown, about 15 minutes. Let cool on a wire rack.

**6 ▲** Meanwhile, combine 1 cup of the strawberries with the confectioners' sugar. Mash with a fork. Stir in the remaining strawberries. Let stand 1 hour at room temperature.

**7 ▲** In a bowl, whip the cream until soft peaks form.

**8 ▲** To serve, slice each biscuit in half horizontally using a serrated knife. Put the bottom halves on individual dessert plates. Top each biscuit half with some of the whipped cream. Divide the berries among the 6 biscuits. Replace the biscuit tops and garnish with mint. Serve with the remaining whipped cream.

~ COOK'S TIP ~

For best results when whipping cream, refrigerate the bowl and beaters until thoroughly chilled. If using an electric mixer, increase speed gradually, and turn the bowl while beating to incorporate as much air as possible.

# Individual Tiramisu

**SERVES 4**

½ pound mascarpone cheese

1½ tablespoons sugar

2 eggs, at room temperature, separated

⅛ teaspoon salt

squeeze of fresh lemon juice

½ cup very strong cold black coffee

2 tablespoons coffee liqueur

1 cup coarsely crumbled butter cookies or pound cake

2 tablespoons unsweetened cocoa powder, sifted

~ **COOK'S TIP** ~

Buying very fresh eggs from a reputable producer is especially important when using them raw.

1 With an electric mixer, beat the cheese, sugar, and egg yolks together until blended and creamy.

2 ▲ In a clean mixing bowl, beat the egg whites with the salt and lemon juice until stiff peaks form. Fold into the cheese mixture.

3 In a small bowl, combine the coffee and liqueur.

4 ▲ Divide half the cookie crumbs among 4 stemmed glasses. Drizzle over 1–1½ tablespoons of the liqueur mixture. Top the moistened crumbs with half the mascarpone mixture. Layer the remaining cookie crumbs, coffee mixture, and mascarpone mixture in the same way.

5 Cover and refrigerate the desserts 1–2 hours. Sprinkle with the sifted cocoa powder before serving.

---

# White Chocolate Mousse

**SERVES 8**

9 ounces white chocolate

⅓ cup milk

1½ cups whipping cream

1 teaspoon vanilla extract

3 egg whites, at room temperature

⅛ teaspoon salt

squeeze of fresh lemon juice

chocolate covered coffee beans, for decoration

1 In a heatproof bowl set over a pan of barely simmering water, or in a double boiler, melt the chocolate.

2 Scald the milk in a small saucepan. Remove the bowl of chocolate from the heat and whisk in the warm milk until smooth. Let cool.

3 In a mixing bowl, whip the cream with the vanilla until soft peaks form. Refrigerate until needed.

4 ▲ Using an electric mixer and a clean bowl, beat the egg whites with the salt and lemon juice until stiff peaks form (do not overbeat or the mousse will be grainy). Fold into the chocolate mixture.

5 ▲ Gently fold the chocolate-egg white mixture into the vanilla flavored whipped cream.

6 Transfer to a pretty serving bowl or individual stemmed glasses. Cover and refrigerate at least 1 hour. Sprinkle with chocolate covered coffee beans before serving.

*Individual Tiramisu (top), White Chocolate Mousse*

# Chocolate Cheesecake

**SERVES 12**

1 pound (16 1-ounce squares) semisweet chocolate, broken into pieces

½ cup granulated sugar

2 teaspoons vanilla extract

4 eggs

3 8-ounce packages cream cheese, at room temperature

2–3 tablespoons confectioners' sugar, for decoration

**FOR THE CRUST**

1 cup graham cracker crumbs

5 tablespoons butter or margarine, melted

2 tablespoons grated semisweet chocolate

2 tablespoons granulated sugar

**1 ▲** Preheat the oven to 325°F. Grease a 9- or 10-inch springform pan and line the bottom with wax paper. Grease the wax paper.

~ **VARIATION** ~

For an all-chocolate cheesecake, substitute an equal quantity of finely crushed chocolate wafers for the graham cracker crumbs when preparing the crust.

**2 ▲** For the crust, mix together the graham cracker crumbs, melted butter or margarine, grated chocolate, and sugar. Pat evenly over the bottom and up the sides of the prepared pan. (The crust will be thin!)

**3 ▲** In a heatproof bowl set over a pan of barely simmering water, or in a double boiler, melt the chocolate with the granulated sugar. Remove the bowl from the heat and stir in the vanilla. Let cool briefly.

**4 ▲** In another bowl, beat together the eggs and cream cheese until smooth and homogeneous. Gently stir in the cooled chocolate mixture until completely blended.

**5 ▲** Pour the chocolate filling into the crumb crust. Bake until the filling is set, 45 minutes.

**6 ▲** Let cool, in the pan, on a wire rack. Refrigerate at least 12 hours.

**7 ▲** Remove the side of the pan and transfer the cheesecake to a serving plate. To decorate, lay a paper doily on the surface of the cake and sift the confectioners' sugar evenly over the doily. With two hands, carefully lift off the doily.

# Coffee Ice Cream Sandwiches

**MAKES 8**

½ cup (1 stick) butter or margarine, at room temperature

¼ cup granulated sugar

1 cup flour

2 tablespoons instant coffee

confectioners' sugar, for sprinkling

1 pint coffee ice cream

2 tablespoons unsweetened cocoa powder

**1** Lightly grease 2–3 cookie sheets.

**2** With an electric mixer or wooden spoon, beat the butter or margarine until soft. Beat in the granulated sugar.

**3 ▲** Add the flour and coffee and mix by hand to form an evenly blended dough. Wrap in a plastic bag and refrigerate at least 1 hour.

**4** Lightly sprinkle the work surface with confectioners' sugar. Knead the dough on the sugared surface for a few minutes to soften it slightly.

**5 ▼** Using a rolling pin dusted with confectioners' sugar, roll out the dough to ⅛-inch thickness. With a 2½-inch fluted cookie cutter, cut out 16 rounds. Transfer the rounds to the prepared cookie sheets. Refrigerate for at least 30 minutes.

**6** Preheat the oven to 300°F. Bake the cookies until they are lightly golden, about 30 minutes. Let the cookies cool and firm up before removing them from the sheets to a wire rack to cool completely.

**7** Remove the ice cream from the freezer and let soften 10 minutes at room temperature.

**8 ▲** With a metal spatula, spread ¼ cup of the ice cream on the flat side of half of the cookies, leaving the edges clear. Top the ice cream with the remaining cookies, flat-side down.

**9** Arrange the cookie sandwiches on a baking sheet. Cover and freeze at least 1 hour, longer if a firmer sandwich is desired. Sift the cocoa powder over the tops before serving.

# Chocolate Mint Ice Cream Pie

**SERVES 8**

⅔ cup semisweet chocolate chips

3 tablespoons butter or margarine

2 cups crisped rice cereal

1 quart mint-chocolate-chip ice cream

3 1-ounce squares semisweet chocolate

**1** Line a 9-inch pie pan with foil. Place a round of wax paper over the foil in the bottom of the pan.

**2** In a heatproof bowl set over a pan of barely simmering water, or in a double boiler, melt the chocolate chips and butter or margarine.

**3** ▲ Remove the bowl from the heat and gently stir in the cereal, ½ cup at a time. Let cool 5 minutes.

**4** ▲ Press the chocolate-cereal mixture evenly over the bottom and up the sides of the prepared pan, forming a ½-inch rim. Refrigerate until completely hard.

**5** Carefully remove the crust from the pan and peel off the foil and wax paper. Return the crust to the pie pan.

**6** Remove the ice cream from the freezer and let soften 10 minutes at room temperature.

**7** ▼ Spread the ice cream evenly in the crust. Freeze until firm, about 1 hour.

**8** For the decoration, use the heat of your hands to slightly soften the chocolate squares. Draw the blade of a swivel-headed vegetable peeler along the smooth surface of each chocolate square to shave off short, wide curls. Refrigerate the chocolate curls until needed.

**9** ▲ Scatter the chocolate curls over the ice cream just before serving.

# Hot Fudge Brownie Sundaes

**SERVES 8**

| |
|---|
| 1 recipe Hazelnut Brownies (page 221) |
| 1 pint vanilla ice cream |
| 1 pint chocolate ripple ice cream |
| ½ cup walnut pieces, chopped |
| FOR THE HOT FUDGE SAUCE |
| 3 tablespoons butter or margarine |
| ⅓ cup granulated sugar |
| ⅓ cup dark brown sugar, firmly packed |
| ½ cup unsweetened cocoa powder |
| ⅓ cup whipping cream |
| ⅛ teaspoon salt |

**1 ▼** For the sauce, combine all the ingredients in a saucepan. Cook gently, stirring, until it is smooth.

**2** Cut the brownie cake into squares. Put a brownie in each of 8 bowls.

**3 ▼** Top each brownie with a scoop of each ice cream. Spoon the hot fudge sauce on top. Sprinkle with chopped walnuts and serve immediately.

---

# Chocolate Cookie Ice Cream

**MAKES 1½ QUARTS**

| |
|---|
| 2 cups whipping cream |
| 3 egg yolks |
| 1½ cups sweetened condensed milk |
| 4 teaspoons vanilla extract |
| 1 cup coarsely crushed chocolate sandwich cookies (about 12 cookies) |

**2** In a mixing bowl, whip the cream until soft peaks form. Set aside.

**3 ▼** In another bowl, beat the egg yolks until thick and pale. Stir in the sweetened condensed milk and vanilla. Fold in the cookies and whipped cream.

**4** Pour into the prepared loaf pan. Cover with the foil overhang and freeze until firm, about 6 hours.

**1 ▲** Line a 9- × 5-inch loaf pan with foil, leaving enough overhang to cover the top.

**5 ▲** To serve, remove the ice cream from the pan and peel off the foil. Cut into thin slices with a sharp knife.

~ COOK'S TIP ~

Buying very fresh eggs from a reputable producer is especially important when using them raw.

*Hot Fudge Brownie Sundaes (top), Chocolate Cookie Ice Cream*

# INDEX

~

## A

acorn squash risotto, 139
anchovies: onion, olive and anchovy pizza, 129
angel food cake, coconut, 196
angel hair pasta with tomato-lime sauce, 120
apples: apple and pear skillet cake, 199
apple pie, 206
apple-walnut crisp, 225
applesauce cake, 202
baked apples with caramel sauce, 226
braised red cabbage with apples, 170
pork chop, potato and apple scallop, 76
asparagus: asparagus, corn and red bell pepper quiche, 180
fried rice with asparagus and shrimp, 142
ham and asparagus with cheese sauce, 84
avocado: avocado, grapefruit and cantaloupe salad, 146
chilled avocado and zucchini soup, 14
Cobb salad, 156
guacamole cheeseburgers, 70
guacamole with cumin tortilla chips, 29
pasta and avocado salad, 154

## B

bacon: pasta with spinach, bacon and mushrooms, 119
spinach and bacon salad, 152
bananas: banana cream pie, 209
banana-pecan muffins, 190
hot spiced bananas, 224
barbecue chicken, 99
barbecue spareribs, 79

basil: pasta with fresh pesto sauce, 116
pesto lamb chops, 86
tomato and basil tartlets, 183
bean nachos, 35
beef: chili con carne, 70
corned beef boiled dinner, 74
guacamole cheeseburgers, 70
layered meat loaf with fruit, 68
old-fashioned beef stew, 72
roast beef sandwiches with horseradish sauce, 26
steak, bell pepper and corn stir-fry, 73
steak sandwiches with onions, 74
steak with spicy mushroom sauce, 68
bell peppers: asparagus, corn and red bell pepper quiche, 180
baked goat cheese with red bell pepper sauce, 178
calzone with bell peppers and eggplant, 130
creamed corn with bell peppers, 162
green bean and red bell pepper stir-fry, 166
pasta with chorizo, corn and red bell pepper, 120
pasta-stuffed bell peppers, 125
pita pizzas, 128
steak, bell pepper and corn stir-fry, 73
biscuits, buttermilk, 192
black and white bean soup, 18
black bean and tomato salsa in corncups, 32
black-eyed peas and ham salad, 155
blinis, buckwheat, with marinated salmon, 30
blueberries: blueberry buckle, 230
blueberry-cinnamon muffins, 190

bourbon sauce, bread pudding with, 234
bread: bread pudding with bourbon sauce, 234
cheesy bread pudding, 182
corn bread, 186
sweet potato and raisin bread, 189
zucchini bread, 188
see also sandwiches
broccoli: broccoli and cauliflower mold, 166
broccoli and goat cheese pizza, 126
brownies: hazelnut brownies, 221
hot fudge brownie sundaes, 250
upside-down pear brownies, 228
Brussels sprouts with chestnuts, 164
buckwheat blinis with marinated salmon, 30
bulgur wheat salad, 136
burgers: guacamole cheeseburgers, 70
lamb burgers with cucumber-mint relish, 90
buttermilk biscuits, 192
butternut squash bisque, 18

## C

cabbage: creamy coleslaw, 148
see also red cabbage
Caesar salad, 150
Cajun blackened swordfish, 45
cakes: apple and pear skillet cake, 199
applesauce cake, 202
carrot cake with cream cheese frosting, 198
chocolate pudding cake, 236
coconut angel food cake, 196
devil's food cake, 194
ginger cake with spiced whipped cream, 200

hazelnut brownies, 221
lemon squares, 220
pound cake, 201
calzone with bell peppers and eggplant, 130
caramel sauce, baked apples with, 226
carrots: carrot cake with cream cheese frosting, 198
carrot soup with ginger, 12
glazed carrots and scallions, 170
casseroles: leftover turkey casserole, 106
noodle and vegetable casserole, 122
cauliflower and broccoli mold, 166
cheese: baby baked potatoes with blue-cheese topping, 28
baked goat cheese with red bell pepper sauce, 178
broccoli and cauliflower mold, 166
broccoli and goat cheese pizza, 126
cheese and dill soufflés, 179
cheese and mushroom frittata, 176
cheese twists with cranberry sauce, 34
cheesy bread pudding, 182
Cobb salad, 156
green bean and Parmesan soup, 16
green salad with yogurt-blue cheese dressing, 150
grilled cheddar and chutney sandwiches, 24
guacamole cheeseburgers, 70
ham and asparagus with cheese sauce, 84
hot cheesy grits, 136
macaroni and cheese, 122
mozzarella, tomato and pesto sandwiches, 20
Parmesan popovers, 193
penne with eggplant and goat cheese, 116
pizza toasts with eggplant and mozzarella, 132

spicy cheese lasagne, 114
spinach and cheese pie, 173
spinach and feta phyllo triangles, 36
cheese, cream: banana cream pie, 209
carrot cake with cream cheese frosting, 198
chocolate cheesecake, 246
cheesecake, chocolate, 246
cherry lattice pie, 212
chestnuts, Brussels sprouts with, 164
chicken: barbecue chicken, 99
chicken breasts with almonds and prunes, 92
chicken-noodle soup, 15
chicken potpie, 100
chicken tacos, 103
chicken thighs wrapped in bacon, 96
chicken with sweet potatoes, 102
club sandwiches, 22
deviled chicken drumsticks, 96
farfalle with chicken and sausage sauce, 118
honey roast chicken, 94
jambalaya, 83
southern fried chicken, 93
chili: chili con carne, 70
chili dogs, 23
turkey chili, 110
chocolate: chocolate cheesecake, 246
chocolate chip and macadamia nut cookies, 217
chocolate cookie ice cream, 250
chocolate mint ice cream pie, 249
chocolate pudding cake, 236
devil's food cake, 194
five-layer bars, 218
hazelnut brownies, 221
hot fudge brownie sundaes, 250

individual chocolate soufflés, 237
Mississippi mud pie, 208
upside-down pear brownies, 228
white chocolate mousse, 244
chorizo: pasta with corn, red bell pepper and, 120
chowder, fish, 54
citrus fish fillets, 46
clams: New England clambake with lobster, 64
club sandwiches, 22
Cobb salad, 156
cobbler, peach, 231
coconut: coconut angel food cake, 196
five-layer bars, 218
cod: breaded fish with tartare sauce, 50
cornmeal-coated cod with tomato sauce, 44
peppercorn-crusted cod steaks, 48
coffee: coffee ice cream sandwiches, 248
individual tiramisu, 244
coleslaw: creamy, 148
roast pork and coleslaw sandwiches, 26
cookies: chocolate chip and macadamia nut, 217
chocolate cookie ice cream, 250
coffee ice cream sandwiches, 248
cowboy, 214
gingersnaps, 214
old-fashioned sugar, 216
pepper-spice, 218
cool and crunchy salad, 147
corn: asparagus, corn and red bell pepper quiche, 180
corn and garlic fritters, 176
creamed corn with bell peppers, 162
pasta with chorizo, corn and red bell pepper, 120
spicy corn salad, 156
steak, bell pepper and corn stir-fry, 73

corned beef boiled dinner, 74
Cornish game hens with cranberry sauce, 98
cornmeal: corn bread, 186
cornmeal and smoked salmon muffins, 32
cornmeal-coated cod with tomato sauce, 44
crunchy corn sticks, 186
fried okra, 162
hot cheesy grits, 136
Indian pudding, 232
couscous with vegetables, 134
cowboy cookies, 214
crab: baked seafood pasta, 124
baked stuffed crab, 56
crab cakes, 56
crab-stuffed cherry tomatoes, 38
cranberries: cheese twists with cranberry sauce, 34
Cornish game hens with cranberry sauce, 98
crunchy corn sticks, 186
cucumber-mint relish, lamb burgers with, 90

D
desserts, 223–50
deviled chicken drumsticks, 96
devil's food cake, 194
dill: cheese and dill soufflés, 179

E
eggplant: calzone with bell peppers and eggplant, 130
penne with eggplant and goat cheese, 116
pizza toasts with eggplant and mozzarella, 132
eggs: Caesar salad, 150
cheese and dill soufflés, 179
cheese and mushroom frittata, 176

Cobb salad, 156
Spanish omelet, 172

F
farfalle with chicken and sausage sauce, 118
fettucine: pasta with fresh pesto sauce, 116
fish: fish chowder, 54
see also cod; salmon etc.
five-layer bars, 218
flans, spinach with tomato-thyme dressing, 174
frittata, cheese and mushroom, 176
fritters, corn and garlic, 176
fruit: fruit kabobs with mango-yogurt sauce, 238
phyllo fruit baskets, 241
tropical fruits in cinnamon syrup, 238
fusilli: pasta and avocado salad, 154
pasta with chorizo, corn and red bell pepper, 120

G
ginger: carrot soup with ginger, 12
ginger baked pears, 228
ginger cake with spiced whipped cream, 200
gingersnaps, 214
goat cheese: baked goat cheese with red bell pepper sauce, 178
broccoli and goat cheese pizza, 126
penne with eggplant and goat cheese, 116
grapefruit, avocado and cantaloupe salad, 146
green beans: green bean and Parmesan soup, 16
green bean and red bell pepper stir-fry, 166
grits, hot cheesy, 136
guacamole cheeseburgers, 70
guacamole with cumin tortilla chips, 29

# H

haddock: fish chowder, 54
halibut: halibut with lemon-pineapple relish, 54
seafood stew, 61
ham: ham and asparagus with cheese sauce, 84
ham and black-eyed pea salad, 155
ham steaks with raisin sauce, 84
hazelnut brownies, 221
honey roast chicken, 94
horseradish sauce, roast beef sandwiches with, 26
hot spiced bananas, 224

# I

ice cream: chocolate cookie ice cream, 250
chocolate mint ice cream pie, 249
coffee ice cream sandwiches, 248
hot fudge brownie sundaes, 250
Indian pudding, 232

# J

jambalaya, 83
jicama: cool and crunchy salad, 147

# K

kabobs: fruit kabobs with mango-yogurt sauce, 238
glazed lamb kabobs, 90
scallop kabobs, 64

# L

lamb: lamb and bean stew, 86
lamb burgers with cucumber-mint relish, 90
glazed lamb kabobs, 90
pesto lamb chops, 86
roast rack of lamb, 89
sesame lamb chops, 88

lasagne, spicy cheese, 114
layered meat loaf with fruit, 68
leftover turkey casserole, 106
lemon: lemon sponge pudding, 232
lemon squares, 220
turkey scaloppini with lemon and sage, 109
lentil soup, hearty, 16
lettuce: minted pea soup, 12
lime meringue pie, 210
lobster, New England clambake with, 64

# M

macadamia nut and chocolate chip cookies, 217
macaroni: macaroni and cheese, 122
pasta-stuffed bell peppers, 125
mango-yogurt sauce, fruit kabobs with, 238
maple-pecan pie, 205
meat see beef; pork etc.
melon: avocado, grapefruit and cantaloupe salad, 146
meringue pie, lime, 210
mint: chocolate mint ice cream pie, 249
minted pea soup, 12
Mississippi mud pie, 208
molasses: Indian pudding, 232
monkfish: paella, 58
mousse, white chocolate, 244
mozzarella, tomato and pesto sandwiches, 20
muffins: banana-pecan, 190
blueberry-cinnamon, 190
cornmeal and smoked salmon, 32
mushrooms: cheese and mushroom frittata, 176
noodle and vegetable casserole, 122
pasta with spinach, bacon and mushrooms, 119

steak with spicy mushroom sauce, 68
turkey Tetrazzini, 110
mussels: paella, 58
seafood stew, 61
mustard: pork with mustard-peppercorn sauce, 76
shrimp in creamy mustard sauce, 62

# N

nachos, bean, 135
navy beans: baked sausages and beans with crispy topping, 82
black and white bean soup, 18
New England clambake with lobster, 64
noodles: baked seafood pasta, 124
chicken-noodle soup, 15
noodle and vegetable casserole, 122

# O

okra, fried, 162
old-fashioned beef stew, 72
old-fashioned sugar cookies, 216
olives: onion, olive and anchovy pizza, 129
omelet, Spanish, 172
onions: baked onions with sun-dried tomatoes, 168
cool and crunchy salad, 147
peas and pearl onions, 164
onion, olive and anchovy pizza, 129
orange: cool and crunchy salad, 147

# P

paella, 58
Parmesan popovers, 193
pasta: baked seafood pasta, 124
pasta and avocado salad, 154

pasta-stuffed bell peppers, 125
pasta with chorizo, corn and red bell pepper, 120
pasta with fresh pesto sauce, 116
pasta with spinach, bacon and mushrooms, 119
see also lasagne; spaghetti etc.
peach cobbler, 231
pearl onions, peas and, 164
pears: apple and pear skillet cake, 199
ginger baked pears, 228
upside-down pear brownies, 228
peas: minted pea soup, 12
peas and pearl onions, 164
pecans: banana-pecan muffins, 190
maple-pecan pie, 205
pecan and scallion pilaf, 141
penne with eggplant and goat cheese, 116
pepper-spice cookies, 218
pepperoni pizza, 130
pesto: mozzarella, tomato and pesto sandwiches, 20
pasta with fresh pesto sauce, 116
pesto lamb chops, 86
phyllo fruit baskets, 241
pies: apple pie, 206
banana cream pie, 209
cherry lattice pie, 212
chicken potpie, 100
chocolate mint ice cream pie, 249
lime meringue pie, 210
maple-pecan pie, 205
Mississippi mud pie, 208
pumpkin pie, 204
spinach and cheese pie, 173
pilaf, pecan and scallion, 141
pine nuts: pasta with fresh pesto sauce, 116
pesto lamb chops, 86
pita bread: pita pizzas, 128
salad-stuffed pita pockets, 20
pizzas: broccoli and goat cheese, 126

calzone with bell peppers and eggplant, 130
mini tomato-phyllo, 133
onion, olive and anchovy, 129
pepperoni, 130
pita, 128
pizza toasts with eggplant and mozzarella, 132
popovers, Parmesan, 193
pork: barbecue spareribs, 79
pork chop, potato and apple scallop, 76
pork chops with sauerkraut, 78
pork with mustard-peppercorn sauce, 76
pork tostadas, 80
roast pork and coleslaw sandwiches, 26
potatoes: baby baked potatoes with blue-cheese topping, 28
mashed potatoes with garlic, 160
new potatoes with shallot butter, 158
pork chop, potato and apple scallop, 76
potato salad, 148
scalloped potatoes, 158
Spanish omelet, 172
poultry see chicken; turkey
pound cake, 201
pumpkin pie, 204

Q
quiches and flans: asparagus, corn and red bell pepper quiche, 180
spinach flans with tomato-thyme dressing, 174
tomato and basil tartlets, 183

R
raisins: sweet potato and raisin bread, 189
raspberries: rice pudding with mixed berry sauce, 240
red cabbage: braised red

cabbage with apples, 170
warm red cabbage salad with spicy sausage, 152
see also cabbage
red kidney beans: bean nachos, 35
chili con carne, 70
chili dogs, 23
lamb and bean stew, 86
red beans and rice, 140
turkey chili, 110
red snapper Veracruz, 52
rice: acorn squash risotto, 139
fried rice with asparagus and shrimp, 142
jambalaya, 83
long-grain and wild rice ring, 138
paella, 58
pecan and scallion pilaf, 141
red beans and rice, 140
rice pudding with mixed berry sauce, 240
saffron rice, 142
risotto, acorn squash, 139

S
saffron rice, 142
salads: avocado, grapefruit and cantaloupe, 146
bulgur wheat, 136
Caesar, 150
Cobb, 156
cool and crunchy salad, 147
creamy coleslaw, 148
green salad with yogurt-blue cheese dressing, 150
ham and black-eyed pea, 155
pasta and avocado, 154
potato, 148
salad-stuffed pita pockets, 20
spicy corn, 156
spinach and bacon, 152
warm red cabbage salad with spicy sausage, 152

salmon: buckwheat blinis with marinated salmon, 30
salmon steaks with lime butter, 46
sweet and spicy salmon fillets, 48
see also smoked salmon
sandwiches: club, 22
grilled cheddar and chutney, 24
mozzarella, tomato and pesto, 20
roast beef with horseradish sauce, 26
roast pork and coleslaw, 26
sliced turkey, 106
steak with onions, 74
tuna and sun-dried tomato, 24
sauerkraut, pork chops with, 78
sausage: baked sausages and beans with crispy topping, 82
farfalle with chicken and sausage sauce, 118
jambalaya, 83
pasta with chorizo, corn and red bell pepper, 120
warm red cabbage salad with spicy sausage, 152
scallions: glazed carrots and scallions, 170
pecan and scallion pilaf, 141
scallop kabobs, 64
seafood: baked seafood pasta, 124
seafood and vegetable stir-fry, 60
seafood stew, 61
see also crab; shrimp etc.
sesame lamb chops, 88
shortcake, strawberry, 242
shrimp: baked seafood pasta, 124
fried rice with asparagus and shrimp, 142
seafood stew, 61
shrimp Creole, 62
shrimp in creamy mustard sauce, 62

smoked salmon and cornmeal muffins, 32
sole: citrus fish fillets, 46
stuffed sole rolls, 51
soufflés: cheese and dill, 179
individual chocolate, 237
soups: black and white bean, 18
butternut squash bisque, 18
carrot with ginger, 12
chicken-noodle, 15
chilled avocado and zucchini, 14
fish chowder, 54
fresh tomato, 10
green bean and Parmesan, 16
hearty lentil, 16
minted pea, 12
winter vegetable, 10
southern fried chicken, 93
spaghetti with sun-dried tomato sauce, 114
Spanish omelet, 172
spicy cheese lasagne, 114
spicy corn salad, 156
spinach: pasta with spinach, bacon and mushrooms, 119
spinach and bacon salad, 152
spinach and cheese pie, 173
spinach and feta phyllo triangles, 36
spinach flans with tomato-thyme dressing, 174
squashes: acorn squash risotto, 139
squid: paella, 58
steak, bell pepper and corn stir-fry, 73
steak sandwiches with onions, 74
steak with spicy mushroom sauce, 68
stews: lamb and bean stew, 86
old-fashioned beef stew, 72
strawberries: rice pudding with mixed berry sauce, 240
strawberry shortcake, 242

sugar cookies, old-fashioned, 216
sundaes, hot fudge brownie, 250
sweet potatoes: candied sweet potatoes, 161
  chicken with sweet potatoes, 102
  sweet potato and raisin bread, 189
swordfish: Cajun blackened swordfish, 45
  swordfish with orange-caper sauce, 42

**T**

tacos, chicken, 103
tartare sauce, breaded fish with, 50
tartlets, tomato and basil, 183
tarts *see* pies
tiramisu, individual, 244
tomatoes: angel hair pasta with tomato-lime sauce, 120
  baked onions with sun-dried tomatoes, 168

black bean and tomato salsa in corncups, 32
cornmeal-coated cod with tomato sauce, 44
crab-stuffed cherry tomatoes, 38
fresh tomato soup, 10
mini tomato-phyllo pizzas, 133
mozzarella, tomato and pesto sandwiches, 20
seafood stew, 61
spaghetti with sun-dried tomato sauce, 114
spinach flans with tomato-thyme dressing, 174
stewed tomatoes, 169
tomato and basil tartlets, 183
tuna and sun-dried tomato sandwiches, 24
tortillas: black bean and tomato salsa in corncups, 32
guacamole with cumin tortilla chips, 29
pork tostadas, 80
tropical fruits in cinnamon syrup, 238

trout, baked stuffed, 53
tuna: tuna and sun-dried tomato sandwiches, 24
  tuna steaks with ginger-soy vinaigrette, 42
turkey: sliced turkey sandwich, 106
  leftover turkey casserole, 106
  roast turkey with Middle-Eastern stuffing, 104
  turkey chili, 110
  turkey Kiev, 108
  turkey scaloppine with lemon and sage, 109
  turkey Tetrazzini, 110

**U**

upside-down pear brownies, 228

**V**

vegetables: couscous with vegetables, 134
  noodle and vegetable casserole, 122
  winter vegetable soup, 10

*see also* asparagus; bell peppers *etc.*

**W**

walnuts: apple-walnut crisp, 225
  upside-down pear brownies, 228
whiskey: bread pudding with bourbon sauce, 234
white chocolate mousse, 244
wild rice and long-grain rice ring, 138
winter vegetable soup, 10

**Y**

yogurt: fruit kabobs with mango-yogurt sauce, 238
  green salad with yogurt-blue cheese dressing, 150

**Z**

zucchini: chilled avocado and zucchini soup, 14
  zucchini bread, 188

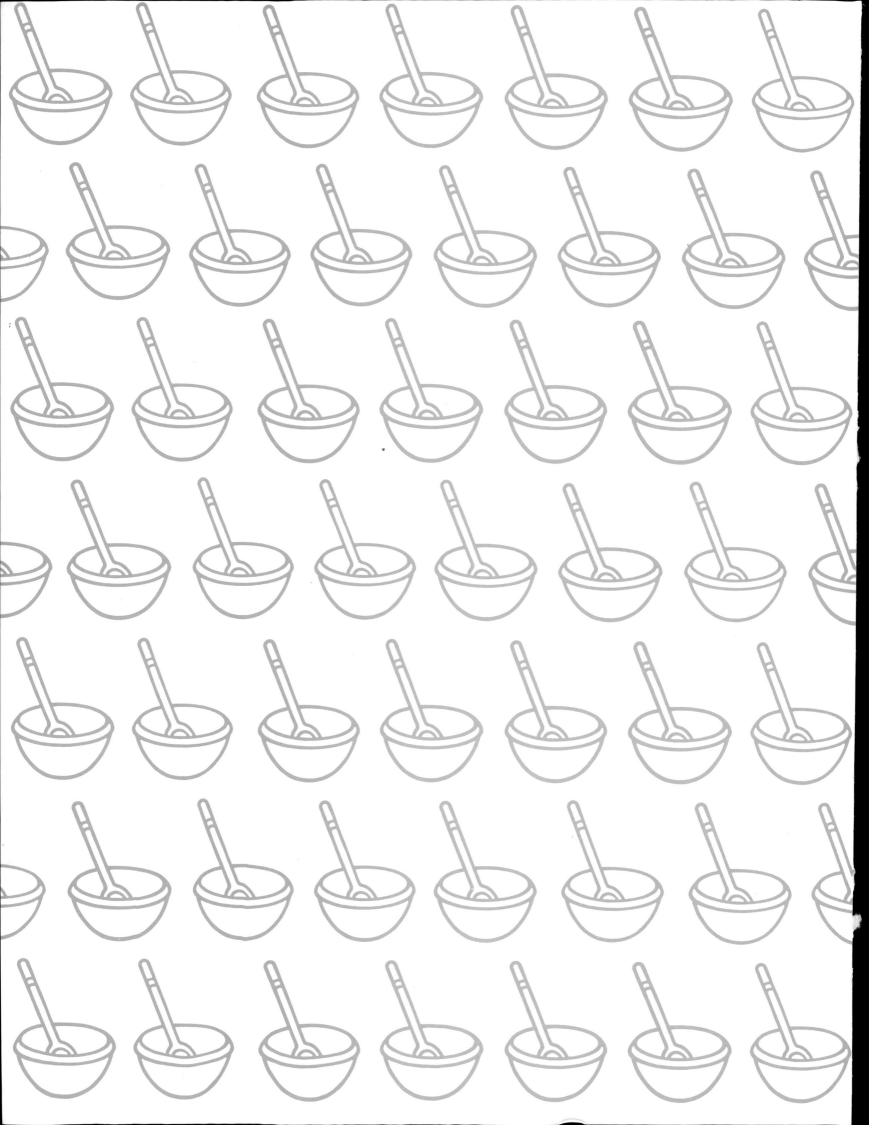